MIRACLES

Karma and Reincarnation Redefined
A Handbook for Purposeful Living

Marian Massie

Copyright © 2024 by Marian Massie

All rights reserved. No part of this book may be reproduced by any mechanical, photographic, electronic process, or in the form of a photographic recording, nor stored in a retrieval system, transmitted, or otherwise copied for public use-other than for 'fair use" as brief quotations embodied in articles and reviews without prior permission of the publisher.

The spiritual teachings mentioned in the text are those derived from the author's personal experience and do not represent the official positions of Eckankar. The intent of the author is only to offer information of a general nature to help you on your quest for spiritual, mental, emotional, and physical growth. In the event you may use any of the information in this book for yourself, which is your constitutional right, the author and the publisher assume no responsibility for your actions.

ISBN: 9798884748248

Editor - Phyllis Mueller, Decatur, GA

Cover and Book Design - Joan Kellogg, Savannah, GA

Publisher - Marian Massie, Pinehurst, NC

MIRACLES

Table of Contents

Copyright	i
Dedication	v
Introduction	vii
Chapter 1 - Understanding the True Profound Purpose of Your Life	1
Chapter 2 - Some Miracles in My Childhood	13
Chapter 3 - How You Create Both Good and Bad Karma	25
Chapter 4 - Easy Tools to Recognize and Heal Emotions That Have Been Negatively Affecting Your Life	41
Chapter 5 - Spirit is Teaching You through Your Daily Life	65
Chapter 6 - Dreams, Their Deeper Purpose, and How to Interpret Them	87
Chapter 7 - Reincarnation	111
Chapter 8 - Freedom and Awareness through Spiritual Exercises	131

MIRACLES

Dedication

To my husband Mark, who has encouraged, supported and helped me to soar.

MIRACLES

Introduction

What is the point and the true, deeper purpose of your life? We live in a time of ambiguity and extremes in every arena. How do you rise above the fabrications and manipulations of social media, news feeds, and podcasts that constantly pound your consciousness?

But where there is darkness there has to be light. Opportunities to excel in awareness have never been greater. The question that arises is how to connect to the illumination.

Through these pages I hope I can ignite a greater light within you and quench your spiritual hunger - a hunger that is rampant in most people, whether they are aware of it or not.

This handbook is designed to answer your questions and give you true, down-to-Earth help for your day-to-day life.

It is populated with stories from my life and those of other people, individuals who gave of themselves from their hearts and to whom I am forever grateful. (And I did change their names.)

You are not alone in your seeking. You are guided always, and now you can learn to recognize and use the spiritual help you are receiving.

Yours in Divine Love,

Marian Massie

MIRACLES

1

Understanding the True Profound Purpose of Your Life

Because you picked this book you are probably looking for answers about your purpose or a deeper understanding of life. Maybe you have already experienced your own miracles, or you believe in karma and reincarnation and want more information.

No matter why you are reading or listening, know there are no accidents in life. You are meant to glean something from this book for your higher awareness that can help you in some way.

This book will take you, step-by-step, to learn how to use your thoughts, beliefs, and emotions in a more transcendent way. You'll discover how to live your life right here, right now as a spiritual experience, a spiritual experience that is different from what you may have encountered in traditional religions or in your investigations so far.

I want to give you understandings and tools to help you navigate your day-to-day living from a higher perspective. I'll provide templates on how to use your daily life occurrences to create and perceive the miracles that are genuinely there for you, to help you unstick negative patterns you may have found yourself in, or to help you raise your level of understanding to what is truly spiritual. So let's begin.

Back in the day, deeply rooted in my subconscious thinking was the belief and hope that one day my life instantly would emerge greater and better through what I came to call a "magic poof." The quick fix mentality that something can change with little or no effort on my part. I hoped an internal switch would be flicked, and poof, I would wake up one day happier and wiser. I think in today's society, many people are searching in vain for this.

Sad to say, the "magic poof" doesn't exist. But what about the title of this book? Isn't it all about miracles? Yes, it is, dear reader. Miracles will emerge in your life through your own undertakings of personal growth because miracles come from your efforts in this life or past lives. You can perceive miracles by you using your consciousness and awareness in expanded ways. You absolutely can learn how to receive and recognize miracles in your life right here, right now.

Let's look at how one dictionary describes miracles.

Miracle-a surprising and welcome event that is not to be accounted for or understood by natural or scientific laws and is therefore considered to be the work of a divine agency.

Miracles seem so biblical, don't they? Things that

happened only to saints and people in the distant past. Wouldn't it be so cool to see and experience your own miracles now? You can! Many people do every day, and I am one of them! I have been guided by Divine agency my whole life.

In this book, I lay out a game plan for those of you who want more out of life, for those who want to connect to something deeper than what society is telling you will make you special or happy.

Or if you just plain want to experience miracles in daily life, doing that takes more than wishful thinking. It takes directed effort, attention, and intention. But experience miracles you can!

First, you must know how life really works.

Imagine you're playing a game but have no idea of the goal or the rules, yet you must play. Think about it. How would you know if you are winning or losing? Incredibly frustrating!

The game goes on, not just for a few hours and not even for one lifetime, but for countless lifetimes. You can never quit the game until you start understanding, integrating, and *living* the rules. Wouldn't you want to know what the rules are and why you are even playing?

Most people stumble about their lives, never understanding what their life is truly all about. The lucky ones create some happiness and purpose. The more fortunate ones connect with the Divine that permeates all of life. Most people, though, work each day just to survive or achieve a modicum of joy.

They live unconsciously, thinking they are in control, but really they are at effect of their past actions, subconscious beliefs, and repressed emotions.

The question of what life is all about never enters their thinking: they don't recognize miracles. The hard struggle of just getting through another day is what most people focus on. Even if you attain every conceivable material goal you have set out to achieve (as the old saying goes) - you can't take it with you. The only thing you can take with you is your state of consciousness.

My spiritual definition of consciousness means the levels of awareness that you as Soul experiences on your journey home to God. In essence your ability to give love and accept Divine Love.

The *Cambridge Dictionary* defines consciousness as "the state of understanding and realizing something." The *Oxford Living Dictionary* defines consciousness as "The state of being aware of and responsive to one's surroundings." and "A person's awareness or perception of something."

This book is about raising your state of consciousness to align it more with the highest consciousness, Divine Love, which is living spiritually. And that state of consciousness you can take with you!

So why listen to me?

In my twenties I learned about the powerful effect of focusing my thoughts to create what I want in life. So for two years, I focused on finding a profession I would love, one where I could help people, one I could do for

CHAPTER ONE

the rest of my life.

Then one day, I had a random conversation with someone about hypnotherapy. Back in the 80s hypnotherapy was in its infancy and not known to many people. But when I heard about it, I was hooked.

Early on, I had realized I innately love to listen to people and help them. I also march to the beat of my own drummer. So becoming something unique like a hypnotherapist and success coach was in tune with my authentic self.

As I learned the deeper meanings and workings of life, I applied that knowledge to what I taught my clients. For most of them I was their last resort after seeing many traditional therapists. The individuals that took what I was teaching to heart started to blossom. Many began observing their lives as an amazing journey.

There are many roads to healing. Traditional therapies, for the most part, just encompass the mind and emotions. In any method of healing, people take away only what they are capable of understanding and are willing to pursue. At different times, in different cycles of life, people need different approaches to grow.

I am trying to impart how the whole game of life is played and provide a guide to help you navigate it more successfully from an elevated perspective. You can use only parts of this handbook or manage your life using all that I am teaching. If you want to open your consciousness to its highest, that means consciously living the reality that you are Soul. And as Soul you get reborn to different lives to learn about love and work off karma. As you go about your life with this knowledge, miracles big and small emerge and become part of your daily life.

This is the superior game. Really it's the only game.

Yes, you are more than this body. Your true self is Soul. You don't possess a Soul, you are Soul.

And why is that important?

Life can be scary and now, especially, world events seem totally out of control. Nature is exhibiting a ferociousness we haven't seen in years. People young and old are taking all kinds of drugs, legal and prescribed, at an alarming rate. The news media pummel the world with messages of fear and greed and doom. (I often tell my clients, the news media are not your friends.) When people are caught up in listening to or watching the news a lot, they often feel depressed or fearful. I give them a challenge. Stop watching the news for a week. See how you feel. My clients that do this feel better because they are not constantly filling their thoughts with an onslaught of negativity.

So how do you make sense of life now? How do you stay balanced and not let pessimism consume your thoughts and be your focus?

Creating new pathways of thinking helps you rise above the massive bleak messages you receive from the media (and probably from your past.) This is the first step to freeing yourself to truly be at cause in your life instead of at effect. Negative thought patterns, whether they originate from your conscious thinking or subcon-

CHAPTER ONE

scious beliefs, create more cynicism and less-than-happy choices, and you become trapped in a spinning gerbil wheel of gloom and unhappiness. At the very least you're not living up to all you can be.

When you start to learn about karma and reincarnation and activate your life each day with this knowledge, miracles start to happen. You can more clearly recognize and unravel your unfavorable patterns of thinking and actions and those of others. I have seen this process work consistently for my clients. Miracles have continued in my life, too. My hope is that by implementing even some of what I am proposing, your life can be transformed into something exceptional.

If you don't know about or understand reincarnation and karma you will keep creating both positive and negative consequences in your life without being conscious of what you are doing. This lack of understanding affects you now and in future lives. Remember the only thing you take with you at the death of your body is your awareness, your consciousness.

You will be like the actor in the movie *Groundhog Day*, reliving the same events over and over. Unless, like Bill Murray's character in the movie, you start to learn from the past and put forth new intentions and actions to create different outcomes.

I don't believe the average person can get out from under all the despair and gloom in this world without a clear, cognizant inner decision to develop a more positive route. This requires working with your thoughts and feelings with a powerful desire to thrive. Thriving means focusing on gratitude, love for yourself and for all of life, and (most importantly) learning to live as your true self, Soul. The mind and emotions can only get you so far.

Maybe you are thinking, "I am not sad or negative." Well, I applaud you, but without directing your life from the awareness that you are Soul, you are destined to keep repeating lower world lifetimes. Think about it, if your true nature is Soul, then learning to connect with your true self helps every part of your life here and now and after your physical body dies.

Yes, I would like to help you to live with the awareness that you are Soul.

You are Soul, living in this physical reality. Most people think they possess a Soul, when the reality is that your true self is Soul having a physical experience. Take a moment now and think. Do you refer to yourself as Soul or do you say you have a Soul? Just shifting your awareness to "I am Soul" can make huge inroads toward a better life, if you allow it.

Why is it important to think, know, and have the perspective that you are Soul?

When you start engaging your life from this consciousness, your life takes on new and more profound levels of reality and clarity. The concepts of karma and reincarnation make total sense, and this awareness helps you navigate your daily life with more love, wisdom, balance, and healing. You begin to see world events from this new perspective. You are less likely to be

CHAPTER ONE

drawn into the drama created by others or to create negative karma for yourself along the way. You realize that your actions do make a difference at a very profound and deep level.

Soul is eternal. YOU are Soul, and hence YOU are eternal. Soul is an individualized, creative spark of God.

If you already believe your life continues after your physical body dies, why is making a decision to embrace the perspective that you are Soul so important? Very simple! Taking action is different from intellectual understanding. For example, you can read about exercise and understand it deeply, but if you don't exercise, you will never get the benefits of exercise, just the knowledge. You have to move your body consistently to reap physical results.

The same is true with accepting and embracing the higher understanding that you are Soul. Living with this understanding means loving yourself even if you make mistakes, uplifting life when you have the opportunity, giving others (who are Soul, too) the freedom to live their unique lives without taking on their responsibilities or engaging in their dramas. (Much more on that later)

It also means taking the time consistently to do some kind of inner spiritual work that helps you connect with your true internal reality. This is exercise for your spiritual self. It elevates every part of your being and can diminish negative karma. You then can begin to recognize the Divine and the miracles in your daily life and be directed and elevated by Spirit instead of being at effect of the lower energies of the world. By connecting more consciously to Spirit you are helping yourself to create more positive karma, in essence freeing yourself from the chains of endless reincarnation.

Miracles are the Divine in communication with you. Connecting with Spirit daily can direct and help elevate you and your life in more profound ways. When I talk about Spirit or the Divine I am not talking about religion per se. Regardless of the path you are on, when you engage in life with the perspective that you are Soul this realization only enhances and deepens what you are practicing now.

Later I'll discuss how to gain a more profound understanding and connection of yourself as Soul and how to work with easy, yet powerful, spiritual exercises to attain this.

Any lifetime is an opportunity, for you as Soul, to develop more Divine Love.

What people seek, whether they realize it or not, is to return to Divine Love, the true essence of all of life, which is eternal and beyond the physical realm.

You are Soul, an immortal being created in the timeless worlds. You existed before birth and endure beyond time and space. God made Soul before the worlds of time and space began.

Soul comes to Earth from the higher spiritual worlds to add to its experiences. It inherits many lifetimes for the chance to learn.

CHAPTER ONE

And learn it must.

Karma and Reincarnation by Harold Klemp, page 1

So you may be wondering now, what does this have to do with you and your daily life?

How is this information going to make one bit of difference in your relationships? How will it help you with your problems or help you to cope with world events right here and now?

Well, I am so glad you asked! If you are open to investigating this way of being, I will show you how this perspective turned my life around and how it continues to help me grow in happiness and compassion for myself and others. I will share some communications Spirit sent me to help me in difficult times. My little miracles, so to speak. I will also share with you some step-by-step exercises to help you change your harmful thought patterns and offer tools to help you heal stuck emotions that keep you creating the same limiting patterns in your life.

But first I will paint you a picture of how my life has been dramatically transformed by living from the awareness that this life is really a spiritual school of growth.

Personal Notes

2

Some Miracles in My Childhood

Everyone's childhood is different. The people in your immediate family will have different experiences than you, even if you were raised in similar circumstances. You are unique. You have had many lives and unique experiences that sum up YOU. To help you understand me a little better, I will tell about some of my experiences. I am the youngest of eight children, raised in the 60s, and I had a very Catholic upbringing. And by very Catholic, I mean my dad went to mass every day and made the whole family say the rosary every night, never asking us if this was what we wanted to do or believed in.

For those of you that are too young to relate, the 60s were a time of strong, authoritarian parenting, yet all around us our world was shifting. New ideas and ways of living were developing. Young people especially were questioning society's values and exploring what they wanted out of life. The Vietnam War was in full swing, and the norms of the 50s were dissolving. Many teens didn't want to follow the dictates of their parents, or to do things just because their mom or dad said so.

I was very much one of those kids.

Being an aware child, I was always trying to make sense of the dynamics of my family, which I now realize was very dysfunctional. The majority of my family issues centered around a very sick mother. One of my first recollections that there was indeed something very wrong was when I was five and my mother was diagnosed with breast cancer. I have a vivid memory of my mom in the kitchen, surrounded by many adults and her having a seizure because of the high dosages of pain medication she was taking. I was horrified and terrified to watch her go through this. My oldest sister Judith tried to comfort me by taking me away from the situation by going to my bedroom and talking to me, trying to comfort me, but to no avail.

I have no memories of my mother before that, and after her seizure I never saw her well again.

My father, on the other hand, was extremely healthy but a typical father of the time. He worked all the time and really didn't know how to connect emotionally with his children or his own feelings. He was raised in the depression in another strict family structure. His father died when he was an older teen and consequently he took over the family meat packing business. His life centered around his work, religion, and occasionally hunting. Never, it seemed, spending quality time with his children. He wasn't a bad man, just emotionally unavailable.

So both my mother and father were not really present. And I didn't receive the emotional bonding children need to get from a parent to feel safe.

CHAPTER TWO

I believe they were good people trying to deal with life the best they could. My mother was always sick. She developed other conditions, such as dependency on valium and alcohol, and was in pain all the time (which we later discovered was from the breast cancer) and was she was understandably depressed most of the time. With all she going through, she didn't have the energy or ability to be a functioning mother.

As for my father, he was always working and was dealing with a very sick wife. He really didn't know how to play with or talk to his children in any meaningful way. This led to my brothers, my sisters, and myself basically fending for ourselves. As the youngest, I got very lost.

By the time I was ten, most of my brothers and sisters were out of the house because they were much older. That left just my brother Michael and myself at home. I took over the household duties. In an unspoken agreement, I did the shopping, cooking, cleaning, and laundry. The four of us were isolated entities trying our very best to survive, never communicating the struggles we were going through. We were taught indirectly not to communicate to people outside our family or to each other about what was going on.

Because I never knew my mother when she was healthy and because she had so many physical issues, I was always fearful my mom was going to die. I became numb, stuffing feelings I didn't know I even had.

A different kind of learning, or how I navigated all this dysfunction.

Since I couldn't or didn't have an adult to turn to, to discuss anything, I turned inward to Spirit. I was always a deeply spiritual person as far back as I can remember, a seeker.

I have a clear memory in elementary school, being on the playground alone, asking myself, "What is life really about?" What kid does that? Through my formative years, I had experiences that taught me the deeper realities of life, even while I dealt with the bitter loneliness I felt each day. Those spiritual gifts helped me to survive.

Being raised Catholic, we were not taught about reincarnation, and awareness of karma and reincarnation was not part of the mainstream culture then. Now it is not uncommon to be introduced to these concepts in books, on YouTube, on social media, and in movies, but that was not the case when I was a kid. When I was about ten, in a contemplative moment, I heard inwardly, *we live more than this lifetime.* I totally comprehended this was true, but I was never taught this. In the depths of myself I just knew.

A life changing and powerful spiritual experience I will never forget, was when I was about twelve. My brother Robert was home from the Marines, in his bedroom, directly across the hall from mine. We were both alone, and our doors were closed.

On this day, he decided to clean his handgun. To be "safe" he thought it would be wise to point the gun inside the house instead of at a window. I don't remember if he knew the gun was loaded. It was. (Of course it

CHAPTER TWO

was.)

I was a very responsible little girl, doing my homework at my desk in my bedroom, when I heard a booming voice scream loudly at me to go sit on my bed, NOW! I immediately obeyed, ran to my bed, and sat. At that exact moment my brother's gun went off. The bullet went through two walls, his and mine. If I had stayed at my desk the bullet would have gone through my temple. As it was, I felt the shot go through my hair and then "kill" a pair of my nicest shoes. I sat there numb. Time seemed to stop.

As loud as that voice was, no one else heard it. It was for me, for my protection. A direct communication from Spirit.

My brother then realized that I might be in my room, and he started to scream my name. I couldn't talk. I really believe now that I was in shock. I never told anyone in my family about the voice. I never shared that story until I wrote my second book, *Dancing with God*.

Hearing that voice yelling at me to protect me was a powerful experience, even though at the time I was too young to process the true and total message Spirit gave me through this ordeal. It helped me on so many levels to realize I am not alone and there is more to this life than this physical reality. What happened to me gave me a deeper understanding of the true Spiritual reality of life. This understanding was not something I garnered from a book or from a source outside myself. It was something no one could invalidate. It was a true spiritual experience. A miracle!

Since I have told this story as an adult, people ask if the voice I heard was one I recognized. (I am assuming they are asking this to see if my subconscious somehow stepped in.) It wasn't any voice I recognized, then or since. But thankfully I obeyed. It was for my highest good at the time.

In looking back at my life, I have to say that was one of the more dramatic assistances I have gotten from Spirit. Most of the time now, they are more subtle, through dreams, waking dreams, or inner nudges. Understand that Spirit, God, or whatever you want to name the energy behind all of life is always talking to us, trying to help us grow for our highest good. You just have to have the consciousness or desire to listen.

Another way the Divine chose to help me as a child (and still does) was through Sound. Spiritual people talk about the Light, but very few know about the Sound. Spirit speaks to us through both.

As a child, many times at night I would hear a humming sound, like high wire electric transmission can make, but there were no high wires around my house. I didn't know what the Sound was and it kind of frightened me. Now I know that Spirit communicates through Light and Sound and when you hear the Sound it is purifying you or helping you in some way. So the Sound I kept hearing as a child was there helping me on an inner level to survive all that I was going through.

The Sounds of Spirit can be varied like the sound of wind, music, water rushing, or buzzing of bees, as well as an assortment of other sounds (which I will get into more depth, later.)

Know when these communications occur you are being nurtured for every part of your reality, cleansed on a spiritual level, and given help for your daily life, even if you don't consciously understand that while it is happening.

Those two incidences with Spirit in my childhood were the more apparent help I received. As I look back, I realize I was always being guided in more subtle ways to help me navigate my loneliness and compensate for the lack of interaction from my parents. Through the massive household responsibilities I took on at the ripe old age of ten, I learned valuable information on how to get things done through my own actions and thoughts and indirectly learned more facets of self-responsibility.

Recall Spirit teaches though daily life actions. You can't change anything in your life without implementing personal responsibility. Despite my own challenges at that young age, I was learning how to let go of being a victim, though I didn't realize it at the time. Letting go of victimhood is paramount in raising your consciousness to a higher place of awareness. My strong sense of accountability got me through some very tough times. I had to sort out, though, not taking on other people's responsibilities.

The Divine also uses other people to help you and teach you lessons that are unique for your life.

I remember being sick a lot during my early elementary school years. Now I understand that I was internalizing much of my mother's feelings and energy. My brother Marty, who was ten years older than I, was quite concerned about my being sick all the time. I overheard him one day telling our mother that the cause of all my sicknesses couldn't be from something physical every time and maybe it had to do with the extensive amount of trauma that was in the family.

What he said really resonated with me, even at my tender age. The miracle for me in this scenario is that as a young child I understood what my brother was trying to convey. It really was a message to me from Spirit to help me navigate my tendency to absorb other people's emotions and energy. I didn't fully learn this lesson until much later, but I don't believe I would have recognized it at all, except that I just "happened" to overhear my brother.

Spirit, I truly believe, used him to get a message to me and help my growth. These are the little miracles I am talking about that go on every day. (I know now that I am an empath. In sick or dysfunctional situations this is not a good trait if you don't have strong energetic boundaries.)

I personally like this definition of an empath that I found on a Google search - **Empaths tend to absorb others' emotions at their own expense when they take on the stress, emotions, physical symptoms, and issues of others as their own. It can therefore be difficult to separate themselves from others, leading to their feeling overwhelmed and burned out.**

As an adult, I have developed strong internal and

energetic boundaries, and I don't tend to absorb other people's energy like I did as kid. I can recognize my feelings and thoughts and separate them from those of other people. Whereas, when I was a child I couldn't discern my feelings from other people's.

Contemplating suicide.

Suicide is the second leading cause of death among people ages 15 to 24 in the United States now. I don't think when I was a teen it was as prevalent. When I was approaching 14 or 15 I remember contemplating suicide. I was a bulimic at that time, very depressed, and drinking and taking drugs. I was just desperately trying to cope.

At a dance when I was 15, I drank so much alcohol and drank it so quickly that I became unconscious and almost died of alcohol poisoning. (Thank God fentanyl wasn't around at that time! If it were, I don't think I would be here now writing this book.) The overt and copious amount of alcohol that I consumed was a very thinly disguised cry for help, that sadly went unheard in my house.

I wasn't consciously thinking of suicide, but I was letting my mind ponder on my death and hoping to somehow end all the negativity I was experiencing. It became evident to my brother Robert that I was in turmoil, though. He was eleven years older than I, and he would occasionally be around the house. He noticed that I was doodling my darker thoughts about death and dying and confronted me about what he found. I was so numb at the time that I had no explanation as to why I was doing this. He even communicated to my mother what he discovered, and told her he was scared that I might commit suicide. What is so heartbreaking about this whole encounter, is that I don't remember anyone talking to me further about this. I was left on my own to flail about.

Your thoughts are not logical when you are deeply depressed and thinking about suicide. What I do remember about that time was looking at a drawer full of butcher knives and wondering if I could use one to kill myself. This was pivotal moment in my life. I remember my inner dialogue. Can I do this? Will I be missed? Maybe I will get their attention if I do this? Maybe then I will be seen.

Remember I knew that there is reincarnation from a very young age. That knowledge was deeply embedded in my psyche. At that point this is where Spirit stepped in again to help me. The Divine whispered into my awareness, telling me what I don't face in this life I will eventually have to face in another and that the learning may be more intense.

I had a choice in that moment: Do I choose life and face what I needed to face, or go through with suicide? (I obviously chose life.)

No family member sat down and talked to me. No therapy was offered. Even though I was depressed Spirit got through to me. And for some reason, I listened.

Instead I chose to run away from home at 15. Living at home was not an option. I was slowly dying there.

CHAPTER TWO

Again my deeply rooted connection to listening to the nudges of Spirit helped me out of a very bad path, this was my inner miracle. My choice was to live, and to do that I *needed* to leave home. Was leaving home at 15 easy? Not on your life. I still went to school, worked three or four jobs, and decided not to live on the street like other teens in similar situations. Through those dark times I only had my intuition and inner nudges from Spirit to help guide me.

I share my stories for the simple reason that I am no different than anyone. We all have problems to navigate in our lives. We are all Soul. It takes an internal decision to live life from the spiritual perspective rather than just the material one. I am sure if you look back on your circumstances and recall the inner nudges you have received, you will realize that you, too, have been guided. The guidance is always there. We just have to develop the awareness to pick it up and use it. The more we tune into it, the louder and more obvious the guidance and nudges become.

The following chapters will help you hone your own development of intuition (inner nudges) through practical and easy methods. Also, I give tools and methods to help you let go of negativity and to create more of what is for your highest and best on all levels, from the physical to the spiritual.

MIRACLES

Personal Notes

3

How You Create Both Good and Bad Karma

Now here's the more in-depth explanation of responsibility I promised you earlier. Each person, each Soul, is responsible for all their actions, reactions, thoughts, and emotions. You are **not** responsible for other people's happiness or problems.

All our thoughts and actions create in each moment. Hence, karma. Karma is just cause and effect. The Bible even mentions it. You reap what you sow. That, boys and girls, is karma.

Imagine a cool game: A world where people take total responsibility for all their actions because they realize on some level, that in this life or a past life, they created the circumstances they are now living through. And it is up to them to change (or not). But only they can change their life. Think about it, there would be no victims. Wow! What a different world we would be living in, huh!

But (you may be saying to yourself) hey, I was abused as a child or attacked as an adult or just in general had a crappy childhood, what about that?

Abuse is wrong in any form. The evil or dishonorable actions of others are not okay. I am not telling you to take abuse.

What I am saying is that to heal, you need to rise above the bad you have experienced in your past. You do this by taking full culpability and accountability of all your actions because in truth some part of you in this life or a past life created everything you go through. To live your life in this manner is the highest form of taking responsibility. This awareness speeds and deepens your healing on every level, emotionally and mentally, as well as impacting other aspects of your life in a finer, higher quality way.

Take whatever bad experience you have had and start transforming your perspective and actions, ask what can you do *now* to help yourself learn from this, instead of staying in victimhood. This is accountability of the highest order. This is how you change negative karma to positive.

For example, when clients come to me about having a bad childhood or some trauma, I try to instill tools and methods for them to take authority for their healing. I ask them, "If you were in a car wreck and you were the passenger, would you just sit there and blame the driver and do nothing, while what you really needed to do is go to the hospital?"

This analogy is in essence what individuals are doing when they stay angry about their childhood or a trauma. The elevated way of living your life is to find ways for you to alleviate the emotional and mental negativity as

CHAPTER THREE

much as you possibly can. That is how you can transform the unfortunate into something more uplifting and constructive.

I want this book to be a guide to teach you a how to heal and elevate every part of your being, in the simplest ways possible.

Even if you don't approach your goals or growth from the highest spiritual perspective, by implementing even some of the teachings in this book, I guarantee you will live your life with more awareness, confidence, and development.

Your first step.

As Soul, you have taken on a physical body, a mental body, and an emotional body to exist here in this physical reality. Each body needs different "foods," so to speak, to be healthy and thrive. Each part of us is really pure energy.

Your physical form needs the right nutrition, exercise, sleep, air, and water to function. You need to process emotions healthfully, instead of denying them, for your emotional body to flourish. Your mental body needs beliefs and thoughts, both consciously and subconsciously, that are good, positive, loving, and uplifting to be its dynamic self.

What follows are some simple, yet effective exercises to help you to recognize your negative or limiting thinking patterns and easy processes to change your thinking to something more uplifting and constructive. I will also assist you to ferret out negative emotions you may be holding onto and tools to help you release or transform them.

On first blush, this may sound complicated, but it can really be quite simple, especially when you realize you have the power within yourself to create the change you are looking for. This handbook will clearly map out the correct tools and direction to help you in your quest.

When I break down understanding myself and how life works, mentally, emotionally and spiritually, it makes investigating what I need to heal and how to transform my awareness so much easier. Understanding yourself and working with yourself is a fluid process. For the sake of ease, I am starting with the mind, both conscious and subconscious, because I imagine the lion's share of people have an easier time knowing what their thoughts are than what they may be feeling.

When my clients come to me for help with a goal or a problem, a great majority of them have never spent focused, quality time to observe their own thought processes. People generally know what they think and thus have beliefs, but to really, closely examine them is something most people have seldom, if ever, done. This is vitally important if you want to take your life to another level of freedom from past or present negativity or to create consciously more of what you really desire.

Your thoughts create, whether you realize it or not, they just do! They are energy. And to gain ground in your life, examining your thoughts is the easiest place to start. Be open to becoming the master of your thinking rather than being affected by your thoughts.

CHAPTER THREE

In his New York Times best selling book, *The Hidden Messages in Water*, Masaru Emote discusses his experiments with distilled water and how the molecules in identical beakers of water changed when he labeled the same beaker of water with different sayings. The water in the beakers with positive sayings attached to them exhibited beautiful white crystals of all shapes, like amazing snowflakes. He put labels on the beakers like "love" and "gratitude," and he had one with the phrase, "I love myself." With each thought the crystals were different but extremely beautiful. Then he put negative sayings on the same beakers that previously had positive labels. Now he had the labels saying "hate," "anger," and "I hate myself." The crystals were no longer white and beautiful. They became dark, muddy, and misshapen. Same water, different thoughts, different results.

He showed that our thoughts do indeed create! Our thoughts create constantly and continually. If you want to change anything in your life, your thoughts are a great place to start.

I challenge you take this first step. Take a hour or a day to observe and monitor your thoughts. Take inventory of what you are thinking most of the time. Are your beliefs positive and loving, or are they complaining, angry, and negative towards yourself or life? Your thought energies will affect your body, emotions, and actions. Part of karma is where you focus your mental pictures. Cause and effect remember? This now (and there is only now) creates your future. Your self-talk, whether you realize it or not, is always creating. I would like you to be in the captain's seat regarding what you want to produce in your life. To do this you have to become aware of what you are thinking and where you focus your thoughts.

When I am in session with my clients, I listen intently to what words they say. If someone repeats a saying over and over, then I know there is a reality behind their words. They may think it is just casual conversation, but in therapy, what clients say are reflections of their true thinking and beliefs.

For example, I had a client that said "I don't know" about 20 times in a one hour session. Ironically, she was coming in to bolster her confidence. Someone who is confident, in my opinion, doesn't say "I don't know" numerous times in an hour. I pointed this out to her and gave her homework: not to say "I don't know" in conversations for the next week. She had to observe her speech, and since this client truly wanted to change, she did her homework. She came back the next week and was blown way by how much more confident she felt. Was this the end of her therapy or the total answer to her lack of confidence? No, but it was a huge first step in her understanding the power within herself to change and create the life she wanted by harnessing her thinking and being aware of what she verbalized.

Your first challenge is to do the same thing. Take a day and observe your speech patterns and internal musings. Record the gist of your thinking, for example, just record the negative stuff: The thoughts that belittle you or others, or what you complain about in your head or voice a lot. The positive and uplifting belief patterns can stay, but you want to be aware of negative ones so you can change them. Know you really can change them, but be brutally honest with yourself, because no one else is going to see what you uncovered. By being truthful with yourself, you will have an accurate starting point for change.

Please don't fall into a trap of putting yourself down for having "Debbie downer" thinking. You are Soul and, hence, you are worthy. Keep in mind you are doing this to change your mental patterns that no longer serve your best interest. Ignoring or pretending the negative is not there will only keep you at your present place. Give yourself permission, with kindness and care, to ferret out what is no longer serving you and inhibiting the directions you want to go.

I continue to monitor my thinking, because I want to be the best me I can be. I can't be my happiest or kindest with destructive or pessimistic thought patterns pulling me down. It bears repeating. Cause and effect, karma, states what you do in this moment you create.

As an older teen, I read the book, *The Power of Your Subconscious Mind* by Joseph Murphy. That book was a stepping stone for me to look more closely at my train of thoughts. I was excited to have a starting template or a road map to change the less than desirable thinking patterns I was holding, not just in my conscious mind but in my subconscious mind as well.

Even through my depression of my late teens and early 20s, I worked to change my mental patterns to empower myself. Since I believed that we are the sum of all the actions and thoughts of this life and all previous lives, I felt truly empowered to work in this moment. I remember thinking, if I created my crappy childhood through former actions, then I can work right here, right now, to create a greater future. You can too, regardless of where you are today or what your past may have been like. The point is to start, right here, right now. Realize there is only now and the power to create is at your fingertips at any present moment!

Some easy ways to change your negative thoughts to positive and uplifting ones.

So if you have done your homework, you have identified at least a few negative or limiting beliefs to work with. I am going to detail an easy exercise you can do to create your goals, whether you want to let go of bad habits or develop more positive karma or a happier path of life.

Writing long hand, and I do mean writing, not typing, on a daily or weekly basis, stating a new goal you want in your life, is beyond powerful. I personally have written my goals for years, but in a different way than you may have heard about. The process of using your hand to write connects you to your subconscious mind more powerfully than typing. I don't know all the science behind it, but I believe putting the physical hand to paper and the movement of the hand creates this connection.

Now on to the process.

A note here on the subconscious mind. The subcon-

CHAPTER THREE

scious mind is 90 percent of your mind power. Unlike your intellect, it has no logic or reason. Think of it as a big dumb computer. Your beliefs about life and yourself have been programmed into your subconscious mind since birth, by how people treated you and what you have been taught as well as the consciousness you brought in from past lives.

You will know what you believe subconsciously by what is *present in your life, not by what you say you want*. For example, if you truly believe that you want a great relationship and you have never had one, you are probably harboring limiting beliefs subconsciously that prevent that reality from manifesting. Your negative self-talk is another indicator of what is embedded in your subconscious. That is why I want you to monitor your negative self-talk.

For this exercise start, with a limiting belief and construct a sentence worded in the present. It's very important that your body also has to feel at ease with the statement. Make sure there is no tightness or sick-to-your-stomach feeling when you read or say the sentence out loud.

Here is a simple example from my own life. I am a golfer. I took up golf, because one day I asked Spirit for a passion that would help me evolve as a person on every level, and the Divine gave me golf! Golf! What a wicked sense of humor Spirit has. (For those of you that don't golf, you are spared from this masochistic game. But I digress.)

A large part of the game is putting. I could drive

the ball, chip, and do decent fairway shots, but for the life of me, putting eluded me. I basically sucked at it. I would approach the ball on the green and hear all my deprecating self-talk. I would hear my internal dialogue repeating "You can't putt" or "You are a terrible putter." When I would think these thoughts I could feel my body become very tense and uptight, which of course didn't help me putt better.

This went on for a long time. One day it occurred to me to start to change my thinking and beliefs about this. It is so obvious to me now, but in the thick of my problem the solution felt like it would never manifest.

(Keep in mind, what I do for a living is to help people direct their thoughts to help them achieve the kind of change they desire. I say this to help you understand sometimes you, too, will forget to use the tools that you are learning here, as I did. Just make use of them as soon as you remember.)

After I recovered from my memory lapse, I went about creating written statements about being the kind of putter I wanted to be. I focused on creating statements or affirmations to let go of the limiting beliefs in conflict to my goal of being a better putter. I wrote the statements in the present tense, and I listened to my body as I crafted them and repeated them aloud.

My creation statements went something like this:

I am feeling safer and safer to be better and better at putting.

CHAPTER THREE

I am worthy of being a good putter.

I let go of my fears and resistances to being a good putter now.

Two of the most powerful ways to start any written affirmations are **safe** and **worthy**. Most people unconsciously feel unsafe to break through old habits of thinking or unconsciously perceive themselves as unworthy, not good enough on some level.

If a statement is right for you now, you can say it out loud and your body will feel neutral or comfortable. If there is internal fear or unworthiness you will feel tightness in your heart area or other parts of your body or feel queasy in your stomach.

Notice that I didn't write, "I am a good putter now," as my first statement. I wasn't ready for that. My body tensed up with that statement, making me realize my whole self didn't believe it or couldn't get on board with creating it. My body also couldn't feel neutral with, "I am safe to be a good putter." I still felt tension, until I wrote the statement, "I am safer and safer to be a good putter." Then my body felt okay. The "safer and safer" was less confrontational for my subconscious mind.

The problem with the way most people go about writing affirmations is they don't take into account how their physical body reacts to the statement. You cannot ram a goal down your mind. If you do, your body and your subconscious will rebel and keep you from achieving your goal. Your physical body's reaction is your unconscious mind communicating your real authentic beliefs through the sensations of your body.

You have to start with exactly where you are, then move forward. After a few days or weeks, your intuition will nudge you when to move ahead. For example, as you write your affirmations after a week or so you may hear yourself saying, "Yeah, I am feeling safer and safer." Then the next step closer to your goal will be using the affirmation with just one "safe." "I am safe to be a good putter." When you feel truly comfortable with that, then the next stronger affirmation is, "I am a good putter."

The same holds true for the other two statements I created for myself. I tested them by saying them out loud and noticed how my body felt. If my body felt tense or resistant in any way to "I am worthy to be a good putter," I backed off and wrote "I am safe to feel worthy to be a good putter," If my body still felt some resistance, I would have backed off again to, "I am feeling safer and safer to feel worthy to be a good putter."

When you work with affirmations this way you speed up the process for your success. Even though part of you may want to go right for the end result, but if you do it that way and the rest of you is not in agreement, I can almost guarantee you will sabotage your progress.

Here's an analogy. Maybe your goal is to run a marathon. The most you have run is a mile or two, or perhaps you have never run before. You have it in your mind to run this marathon, so without training, you pick a day and run. You won't get very far, and it's very likely you will incur injuries. The quickest and most effective

CHAPTER THREE

way to reach your goal of running a marathon is to start where you are physically and then slowly increase your distance. This method helps your body get stronger. As you gradually increase your mileage you experience the reality that you can, indeed, accomplish this.

As you work with your creation statements from where you are, observe how your thinking changes and what actions you may take that are different, yet reinforce your end result. Like me with the putting. I felt calmer on the green more often. I also experimented with a totally different style of putter that proved really helpful. All these inner and outer changes began when I started writing my goals. Now my putting has improved dramatically. I am no longer nervous or tense when I go to putt. I am just having fun!

To complete your understanding of how to write affirmations, I must mention one more thing that may be keeping you back. That's fear. Letting go of fear can be an interesting process. If, for example, you have tried to create an affirmation with the word "safe" or "safer and safer" and your body still is tense, then there is a part of you that is still invested in keeping the fear. This sounds illogical (and it probably is) because emotions are not governed by logic.

To begin to release this fear, make a creation statement that addresses the fear first. As an example, I will use the putting illustration. If, when I said, I am "safer and safer to be a good putter" and I still felt tense, then I would have to address the fear first. The creation affirmation would then be," I am safer and safer to *let go* of my *fear* of being a good putter." I would write this until I felt calmer, and then step-by-step I would use the other statements.

When you take control of what your mind thinks and the direction of your thoughts, you are being at cause instead of effect. You are taking a big step forward in refusing to be bandied about by life, going where the wind blows you or staying a victim from your past. You are starting to reshape your karma. In later chapters that deal with getting in touch with yourself as Soul, I will provide more tools to help you let go of negative karma and help create more good karma, which in turn affects every part of your life. For now, let's focus again on the mind or the thinking part of you.

Another very powerful way to create what you want with affirmations is to take one affirmation and write it 15 times once a day. I have written affirmations both ways and they both work. The 15 times version speeds up the process, but you must have a statement that feels good in your body. When I did the 15 times way, I would number the page 1 through 15 and just get to work.

Each day that you do this, look for subtle changes in your thinking and actions. Maybe you write down, "I am safe to heal my hip injury." After a few days you may have a conversation with a friend that just "randomly" tells you about this fabulous physical therapist. This could be Spirit speaking to you, giving you a nudge to try this approach in your quest for healing. Maybe you notice your self-talk is more positive or you read something about a food or supplement that is good

CHAPTER THREE

for your particular issue.

With creation statements you set up the energy to come to you. You then need to listen and take physical actions to make the goal a reality. It might take many steps along your journey of growth. Keep taking internal inventory on your progress, and graciously accept help as it is given. Goals may be reached in days, weeks, or longer. When you consciously work with Cause and Effect it becomes exciting to see that, as you continue to focus your actions and thoughts in the direction you want to go, miracles start to show up, both large and small. Gradually you will get better at recognizing the gifts of Spirit as you put effort into your own growth.

Personal Notes

4

Easy Tools to Recognize and Heal Emotions That Have Been Negatively Affecting Your Life

---

Ah, what fun! On to emotions! What a tangled web we weave when we deceive ourselves, knowingly or unknowingly, regarding what we really feel.

You really cannot escape your emotions. You can bury them, pretend they are not there, or project them on to others, but those little devils are with you until you decide to face them. Even buried, they affect your decisions, actions, and general well-being.

It is important to recognize that emotions are energy, too, and energy creates whether you are conscious of it or not. By facing and healing emotions that have been impacting your life, you free yourself of more negative karma. Why? Because you are no longer at effect of your hidden feelings.

Even if you don't buy into the concept of karma, why is it important to face your anger, frustrations, feelings of not being good enough, sadness, fears, or grief?

What are the benefits? There are two major reasons or benefits for facing your emotions and handling them in healthy ways.

One benefit is that by confronting them (or in therapeutic terms, processing them in such a way that they are no longer the driver of you) your confidence grows and you can live as a more authentic, aware self, right here and right now.

The second reason, and for me the most important one, is to evolve your awareness that your truest self is Soul. Living in the quagmire of being at effect of your subconscious beliefs or your emotions or keeping yourself on an endless loop of reacting to situations, prevents you from being free, truly free. As Soul you are free in the truest sense of the word and by doing this work you whittle down the chains of cause and effect (karma) that keep you coming back to this Earth lifetime after lifetime.

Regardless of why you choose to work with your feelings, you absolutely will come out stronger, more aware, and less reactive. This, in turn, makes your relationships healthier, more authentic, and joyful.

A story of repressed anger killing a man's business.

Let me tell you two stories that point out exactly what I am trying to convey regarding how repressed anger can create roadblocks to happiness.

I had a client who was a confident businessman. He knew his craft, yet he was self-sabotaging his business

CHAPTER FOUR

to the point where he would lose it if he didn't start to market his business. Much to my surprise, he told me he was spending all his work time playing video games!

I asked him what he did, and he told me he was a CFO consultant. Then, through a series of questions, I discovered his serious lack of motivation started after he was fired from a previous company. He told me the company's owners wanted him to "cook the books," or in other words, be dishonest, and he refused. The next thing he knew he was fired. That is when he decided to go out on his own, and that is also when he started to self-sabotage his business. He was manifesting all the symptoms of repressed anger.

Please recall, all emotions are energy, and they produce effects in your life whether you are conscious of them or not. If they are hidden or repressed, then more likely than not they will generate issues in your life that you really don't want.

I told him we would work on his suppressed anger first. He vehemently stated he didn't "feel" angry. I said, "Of course you don't, it's in your subconscious. Your anger is hidden from your conscious awareness, but it is definitely affecting your actions." He told me he felt like he had dealt with his anger with logic and reason, truly both good places to start. The truth of what is working, though, is always revealed through actions and reactions to what is actually happening. I pointed out to him, if he actually had released the anger through logic and understanding, he wouldn't be now experiencing the lack of motivation.

Reluctantly, he agreed to let me help him process his anger. I did this through imagery and dream suggestions. In that first session I did nothing to suggest a greater action to build his business, we just worked on moving anger energy out of his consciousness. He came back the next week and said his motivation increased 50 percent, and he was actually marketing his business.

I truly believe that if he never got in touch with and released his unconscious anger, his business would have failed.

My story with subconscious anger.

My childhood was overlaid by my mother's many illnesses and her struggles with drugs, alcohol, and depression. I loved my mother, and she was a good person, but with many huge challenges. I was an astute kid and I understood she was doing the best she could. (To those of you coming from hard childhoods, does this sound familiar?)

No one helped me recognize that even though I understood what my mother was going through, it would have been natural and normal to be angry about her being sick all the time, her drug and alcohol dependencies, and my not getting the nurturing from her I needed as a child.

Consequently, I ended up stuffing or repressing all my anger. How could I be mad at a sick person and feel good about myself? I was stymied. I mostly felt numb. Subconsciously, I felt guilty for being angry at my mother.

CHAPTER FOUR

Repressed emotions can impact your physical health as well. Consequently, due to my pent up anger, I got sick a lot. One year in elementary school I was sick with colds and vague illnesses that kept me out of class for a total of almost six months. I also became bulimic at age 14, throwing up six to 10 times a day. And hey, I was depressed, too, and becoming suicidal. A smorgasbord of life-sucking issues. Recall subconscious, repressed anger creates depression, low self-esteem, and self-sabotage and can affect your physical health. Stuffed deeply enough and unresolved, it can lead to suicide. I was batting a thousand.

Realizing I was becoming suicidal, to prevent myself from following through with this, as a deterrent, I chose to run away from home at 15 instead. Somehow, I had the intestinal fortitude to go school, work, and get my diploma. I definitely believe Spirit helped me through the dream state to maneuver through these incredibly tough times. I literally had no one to turn to. Through my teen years and into my twenties I remained bulimic. That, too, got resolved after I began in earnest a daily spiritual practice in my late twenties. But when I was 14, no one had heard about or knew how to deal with bulimia. So I was left, yet again, to deal with my bizarre behavior on my own. Part of me thought I was kind of crazy, but not really mentally ill. I was alone with this huge secret that required an incredible amount of energy to keep hidden and to navigate daily life.

But step-by-step I was gaining a foothold in my life, learning how not to be affected by my past and to be the captain of my thoughts and emotions instead of just reacting to them. I really embraced the concept of focusing my thoughts toward what I wanted and not dwelling in the negative or what I didn't want. My self-esteem, as a result, started to get better. Thus, day-by-day, I created a better future by changing my beliefs and healing my emotions.

Even though I was seeing progress in my life, I still remained bulimic until I was 24. Ever the seeker, my spiritual searching led me to Buddhism, the kind where I could still wear makeup, lol. This form of Buddhism taught me I am totally responsible for all my life and that Spirit communicates to us through Sound as well as Light.

Through my spiritual searching, I discovered quite quickly that silent meditations didn't suit me, as I would fall asleep. It's hard to gain traction in your life when you are snoozing! This particular Buddhist practice taught to use a mantra and to repeat it out loud. Working with a mantra turned out to be a good fit for me. A mantra is a high vibratory word that feeds you from a spiritual level and helps you to raise your consciousness above all the worldly negativity. Some mantras, though, reach you deeper and more profoundly than others.

After 14 years of throwing up multiple times a day, I had given up all hope of ever overcoming bulimia. The only reason I started to chant my mantra daily was to connect to Spirit, and frankly, to get some feeling of normalcy in my daily life. I was profoundly depressed at that time and I found out this was the only thing that lightened my heart even a little and made daily life more

CHAPTER FOUR

bearable.

I would chant every day until I felt an inner shift, a lightening in my heart. I never once asked for or even expected a healing. After a month, though, my depression started to lift and my bulimia completely went away! It has never returned.

My action of implementing something that raised my consciousness also healed the repressed anger that was causing my bulimia and depression. I still do a Spiritual exercise every day, now to become a more loving person and to connect more deeply to my true self as Soul.

I hope this story was not too long-winded. I wanted to show how you can detect hidden emotions from the past or the present. By allowing yourself to know what you honestly feel about situations and what is actually occurring in your life, you can get a clearer understanding of what you need to do to heal and excel. Through transparent honesty with yourself you can have the starting point, direction or your roadmap to reveal a greater you.

Some answers are easy and relatively quick, like the situation of my businessman client, and some, like in my situation with bulimia, take much more time and effort to heal. But boy is it worth it! I liberated myself from the prison of bulimia and depression. I have been told that being free of severe bulimia without therapy after fourteen years was a miracle. I must admit it felt like one to me.

I hope you are beginning to see more completely

how powerful your subconscious or stuck emotions can be, and how they absolutely impact your life, usually not for the better. Please do keep all the joy, gratitude, and love that you can instill in your life. I hope to help you recognize, allay, or move through only negative emotions. I will give you tools you can implement to help alleviate your anger and other emotions, such as fear and unworthiness.

Start with anger first, as I have seen in conducting therapy that most, if not all, people are bandied about by inner anger in some form or fashion. When you get comfortable with working with anger, you can apply the same techniques to fears, shame (which is condensed unworthiness) sadness and grief.

I have to recommend the book, Homecoming by John Bradshaw. He has passed on, but he, in my opinion, is the grandfather of helping individuals recognize and heal unconscious emotions, such as anger and shame. He has many talks on YouTube that are a great resource of healing, too.

Understanding anger as an energy.

Being human, you will have experienced anger in some form. Some anger is hidden from your consciousness but other forms of anger are more apparent. It's how you deal with it that is the most important. People generally do not want to admit they feel angry. Maybe it's because of how they were raised, or maybe they feel that they are not a good person if they feel anger. Consequently many people deny it.

CHAPTER FOUR

Think of anger energy on a continuum, from super stuffed and mostly invisible or unapparent to being out there in all its nasty, for others to see.

The symptoms of hidden anger include frustrations and irritations, which are all part of what I call the anger family. Hidden anger can also manifest as depression, lack of motivation, low self-esteem, and self-sabotage. (To clarify, self-sabotage is when you know what to do but you consistently don't do it and it impacts you in a negative way.)

Symptoms of anger on the other end of the spectrum would be projecting your anger on others. This can include persistent snide or sarcastic humor, consistently being argumentative, yelling or raising your voice, and, of course, physical violence.

Reasons you hold on to anger.

There are four main reasons you hold onto anger.

1. The need to punish yourself or others.

Let's look at what the need to punish really means. Two examples come to mind. The first example could be when a romantic relationship ends badly. Maybe you broke up with them or they broke up with you. It doesn't really matter who broke it off, the feelings of anger are still present within you. The inner message you tell yourself is you have been wronged in some way, shape, or form.

You are angry. You may have lost your dream or your companion, and you may have been hurt. Probably you don't even realize that you want the person chastised or disciplined for hurting you. This, my friend, is what the need to punish looks and feels like.

Another example, which may be more subtle, is when you have come from a dysfunctional childhood. Maybe your parents or siblings didn't give you the love, nurturing, or healthy mirroring you needed to be happy. Because you are smart, you realize, maybe through therapy, that your family did they best they could, but every time, or a lot of the time, when you talk to others about what you didn't get from your childhood, anger, irritation, or hurt surfaces when you speak.

When you do, perhaps you raise your voice when speaking about the loss you had, or you start to feel tension in your body. You might even imagine telling off or trying to educate your family members about your suffering in order to get them to change. This, too, is the need to punish or in other words, teach someone a lesson. Deep in your mind you believe if they get their lesson or punishment then you can move on.

But it's just the opposite. When you let go of your need to punish anybody or anything, your internal anger will go away. Then you truly can move on with more peace and healing.

I mentioned hurt here with anger because you may be so out of touch with your anger that you substitute saying you are hurt instead of angry. For a lot of people having hurt feelings is a more acceptable way to think about a situation than truly admitting they are angry. But not becoming conscious of angry feelings keeps you stuck. Acknowledging anger gives you a direction for transformation. Know and realize all your emotions are ok. They are part of the human makeup. How you deal with them is what makes the difference in your life.

2. Anger keeps you tied to the person or situation.

Picture yourself angry at something, perhaps a world event or something someone said on social media. Now visualize yourself constantly going over and over the insult or the terrible issue. Look, see, and notice that more you engage, even in your thoughts, the greater the situation grows in your consciousness. You probably feel your anger mounting, also.

Energy creates, so when you consistently focus your energy on your anger the longer it stays in your life, your body, and your mind. You basically draw the situation you are angry about to you by keeping your resentment alive. Ask yourself this question. Is this really what you want to keep creating?

3. Anger keeps you from facing your own stuff, thus maintaining your victimhood.

I think I am like most people, it is hard to be objective about yourself. So what I am going to say next may hurt a little. At any given time you are either living as a victim or choosing to work on developing your life with more awareness regardless of what happened in the past or what's happening in the present.

I am all for the occasional pity party, but when it becomes part of your routine to keep adhering to the low vibrations and actions of complaining, wallowing in your hurt, not taking responsibility to change your circumstances or inner thoughts and feelings, you are living in victim consciousness. Staying angry at circumstances, past or present, keeps you tied to staying trapped and powerless.

If you choose to put effort into letting go resentment, exasperation, and annoyance, you will find expanded inner peace, enhanced confidence, and greater personal empowerment. That's totally the opposite of being a victim.

4. It's the way you learned to survive emotionally.

You are taught how to respond to life, people, and circumstances from the time you are born. For example, if your parents treated you with love, care, and respect, then you probably have a good foundation to handle life as an older child, teen, and adult and possess good emotional tools to deal with life's circumstances. If, on the other hand, you had trauma (such as I did with a sick parent) or experienced violence or abuse in its many forms, then you may have taken up the sword of anger, internally or externally, to keep yourself alive mentally, emotionally or physically. A big part of being human is the instinct to survive.

What we cultivated as a way to handle and get through and survive hard situations in the past is what we will invariably keep using in the present, even if a situation is not warranted.

For example, maybe you know someone that seems

CHAPTER FOUR

to overreact to average situations with criticism, yelling, or aggression. That is the person's subconscious survival instincts kicking in, their learned behavior. On the other end of the spectrum, repressed anger is also as a way to survive. Maybe when you were growing up you never felt safe when you expressed anger. Or you witnessed other people who got punished or unloved when they expressed anger. So you chose subconsciously to repress anger feelings to avoid emotional abandonment or physical punishment. Depression, then, can result from anger that you have never dealt with. Other red flags that you have not dealt with anger are often manifested in self-sabotaging behaviors that impact the quality of your life, like consistent overeating, persistent over imbibing in alcohol, using drugs or over spending.

Now that you know major reasons you may be holding onto anger and how it may manifest, what do you do with this information?

Ways to release anger and the patterns that hold anger in place.

Now you that are starting to recognize anger in its many forms and patterns, you can start to clear away your anger energy and how it has affected your behaviors. If you are depressed, you can start by saying, I probably have repressed anger. You then can look back at your life, and recognize when it started, and work from there.

I know it is a cliche, but start with your childhood and work forward if you have been depressed for a very long time. Or look at life-changing situations such as losing a relationship (pet or human), a job, moving, or betrayals, or traumas and work from that point.

In my book You are Soul, I write about many tools for removing anger. Here are a few.

1. Write an anger letter to the person with whom you are angry.

Never give them the letter. This is a process for you, to let yourself become more conscious of your true feelings and to ultimately process them. When you do, you hopefully will be able to let go of the anger you have been holding onto.

Approach your writing with the true intention of *letting go* of your anger, not reliving it. If you do it from this perspective you should feel lighter, clearer, and freer. If you do not, some part of you still wants to hold on to this anger, probably to punish the person or situation. If so try the writing exercises that are detailed next, to release the need to punish.

2. Working with affirmations to release anger and your need to punish.

Let's look at how this would work. Start with the number one reason most people hang on to anger is the need to punish. Writing affirmations can help you let go of this subconscious need. Here are some examples of affirmations that give you the most bang for your time. Write a few and notice the change in how you feel or think in the next few weeks.

Yes, I said, weeks. This is a process, but not linear

CHAPTER FOUR

in nature. Let's say you have been depressed for 10 years. If you work the processes outlined in this book, it shouldn't take 10 years for you to grow and change, but it does take effort, intention, and consistent action. Many of my clients experience positive developments in a few weeks, even if and they had been angry most of their lives.

Try some of these creation statements. Please say them out loud first and notice if they feel comfortable or neutral in your body before you spend a lot of time writing them.

I feel safe to release the need to punish _____.

I am feeling safer and safer to release the fear of letting go of my need to punish _____.

I am safe to let go of my anger regarding _____.

I am safe to let go of my fear of letting go of my anger regarding _____.

I replace my anger with healthy boundaries and self-worth and inner peace.

Try working with a combination of these affirmations. The first four are about letting go of anger and the need to punish; the last is returning to a healthier and higher way of living. Rule of thumb, when you let go of something with writing or visualization, always, as a second step, put something more positive and uplifting back into your consciousness. Nature will fill up a vacuum, usually with the stuff you are trying to let go. So if you don't consciously fill yourself with something healthier and more positive, the old stuff will likely come back. Examples of ways to fill yourself up with superior options would be to imagine love, gratitude, and self-worth nourishing you.

Working with your imagination.

1. Healing Spa.

Imagine you are approaching a shimmering, golden building. Maybe your guardian angel or spiritual guide is with you to support you. Everything about the structure vibrates with warmth and love. You feel completely safe and comfortable here. You open the golden door and enter. In front of you is a beautiful whirlpool of turquoise light. You step into it. The light passes through you, releasing anger and any negativity you are holding. Know you are absolutely secure to relax. The light gently flows through your body pulling out of you the anger that you are inwardly holding onto. Visualize the anger as darkness. Now visualize it away from you, gathered at the other side of the whirlpool.

Next, when you are ready, get out of the whirlpool and go across a hall to a large room with a high, domed ceiling. A pale blue or yellow light emanates throughout the room. You notice a fluffy white bed and you lie down on it. Now breathe deeply and slowly, allowing both the blue and yellow light to enter you and fill you up with balance, healing, and love. Realize you can come back here anytime through your visualizations and in your dreams, letting go of anger and the beliefs that have kept the anger in place.

CHAPTER FOUR

2. Separating from a negative relationship or circumstance.

Many times we hold onto anger because certain relationships or situations get stuck in our mind or emotions. For instance, maybe a relationship or a job you wanted either ended badly or you never got it in the first place. Or perhaps you relive something from your childhood over and over again with anger, feeling like a victim. If these situations are something you have experienced, try this visualization.

First get yourself into a higher vibration or consciousness by chanting HU, which sounds like the word hue. You sing it on an elongated out breath, like HUUUUUUU. This is an ancient name for God, and chanting it raises your awareness and consciousness. (Remember, you are working on letting go of anger to create better karma and a greater or more advanced way of living your life. And you can't do this when you are stuck in anger.) Singing HU infuses your visualizations with help from Spirit regardless of your spiritual path or lack of one. Please do not direct the HU. Just sing it for a few moments, then proceed with the exercise.

Also *all change in your life starts within yourself.* As you change your thoughts, energy, and focus, you are actually changing your consciousness. That impacts your physical reality, and for the better.

So after you have sung HU for a few moments, imagine yourself standing in front of a dark picture and place the person or situation you are angry at in the dark picture. You are surrounded by the Light of Spirit and are thus absolutely secure. Take a balloon from your pocket and breathe into it all your stuck anger. The balloon can get as large as you need it to be.

When you feel even a small shift in your body, like a lightening in your heart or feeling of calmness, then with intention and attention, let the balloon go. By doing this you are releasing your anger to the Universe or Spirit, whatever you are in in-sync with. Now breathe deeply and slowly.

Look at the person or situation you have placed in the picture, notice the picture getting lighter. Next, reach inside yourself and pull out any negative beliefs or emotions you may have absorbed from them. Say, "I am giving these back to you." Present them with those beliefs and emotions.

Now, reach inside them or the situation and say, "I am taking back my power I may have given you." Reach inside them, pull your power out, and put it back into you.

Imagine now that a loving being comes and hands you a golden sword of light. You pick it up. Notice there was a dark cord of energy connecting you with the person or situation that you placed in the picture. Take a deep breath and cut the cord. See and imagine the person or circumstance separate from you.

Next, you turn in the opposite direction, which is your present or your future, and visualize yourself happy, balanced, and at peace. Imagine a beautiful golden or white light connecting you to this new state of being.

CHAPTER FOUR

Take several moments to allow yourself to deeply receive this higher way of living.

Why heal your childhood wounds?

If we are honest, we all carry around wounds from childhood. You may tell yourself, "Well, this is in the past and I am over it," but you may or may not be. If you are not truly over your childhood wounds, then your past is actively affecting your present.

Ask yourself, does your body tighten up when you think about what happened to you as a child, adolescent, or teen? Have you had unexplained feelings of not being good enough or feeling less than or prolonged feelings of emptiness? When you talk about your childhood to others does anger come to the surface about what you didn't get or what may have happened? Or are you numb? (Numbness is another indicator that you are not dealing with your negative past because it was just too overwhelming.)

You may be thinking, "I don't want to rehash the past or blame anyone, I want to get on with my life." This is all well and good, but the subconscious always functions from this now and has no logic or reason. If you have wounds that are not addressed and cleared, they are with you in this now, this today, and in your future, and they keep creating karma.

Or you may be someone who sees how prolific victim consciousness is in our society today. You don't want to be one of "those" people who blame their parents, their childhood, or whatever for all their problems. I applaud you if you are one of these people, but be aware that if you don't consciously confront the hurts that are still in your subconscious, you are still being affected by them, in some way, shape, or form.

I am asking you to adopt a more advanced way of looking at responsibility, if you so choose. By doing so, you can free yourself on all levels that have been affected by past mental and emotional wounds by confronting the feelings and the negative beliefs you still hold. By doing this work you can liberate your mind and emotions. Then you can operate your life with a clearer perception, and even soar to new heights of joy.

An exercise to help heal childhood wounds.

Please approach this visualization from your heart as much as you can. The place I would love you to go to is the feeling you get when you connect with your pet or the feeling you get when you send love to your young children or nieces and nephews or a loving partner or a great friend.

With that feeling of love, imagine, your inner child is in front of you. That part of yourself that got lost, abandoned, hurt, or was unloved. Look that child straight in the eyes and with feeling and say in your imagination, "I am here for you now, I refuse to abandon you for any reason, and I love you."

Many different emotions may surface at this point. Breathe through them and think of the process as detoxification of your emotional body. Do your best to keep the connection to your little inner self.

CHAPTER FOUR

Next, imagine you are pulling out anger, unworthiness, sadness, and fear from your youngster. See all the emotions as dark goo. Pull those energies out of your inner child's head, heart area, and stomach. Pile up all that ick.

When you are done, take your child's hand and walk over to a gallon of gasoline. Pick it up and pour it over the black pile of gunk that you stacked and accumulated.

Now both of you step back to a safe distance, light a match, and throw it on that dark pile. Watch it ignite and burn up completely.

Imagine next a beautiful, light, maybe it is white, blue or yellow, entering you and your inner child, filling you both up with healing, Divine Love, inner security, and self-worth. Breathe in the light and relax into it. Practice accepting it into your whole self.

After you have accepted as much positive light as you can, look into your little one's eyes and say from your heart, "You are good, worthy, and safe to feel safe, and remember I am always here for you."

Do this exercise daily until you feel stronger inside and you can connect to your inner self with love and acceptance.

Any of these written or visualization exercises can be used to address any emotion you are having a difficult time with. For written affirmations replace anger with fear, guilt, unworthiness or whatever emotions you need to work on. The same substitution process is true regarding visualizations.

A recap.

Your true nature or self is Soul. You take on a physical body, an emotional body, and a mental body to navigate this reality. In my opinion, karma affects your life whether or not you believe in reincarnation. If these concepts are too out there for you, that is absolutely ok. You can still empower yourself by living your life more mindfully. One way is by recognizing when your thoughts and emotions are limited or negative. Now you have tools you can use to change them and to become more empowered and free.

Thoughts and emotions are energy, and they create everything in your life. So by observing and choosing to instill more uplifting beliefs and emotions, your life absolutely will change for the better. You now have methods and tools to heal and release the emotions and the beliefs that cause you discomfort or suffering.

My goal is to help you become the captain of the ship that is you. As the captain you have the freedom to go as far as you like on your journey of awareness. If you want to go deeper and further, please read on. You'll learn more in-depth about karma, reincarnation, past lives, karmic ties in relationships, the spiritual power of dreams, and Soul travel. Regardless of your religious or spiritual inclination, what you learn can impact your personal life journey so that you can soar to new heights.

CHAPTER FOUR

Personal Notes

Personal Notes

5

Spirit is Teaching You through Your Daily Life

With every lifetime you learn through each and every experience and relationship. What you learn is up to you. Think of each past life and this present one as your personal school. What do you want to learn? In truth, there are only two choices: power or love. You may think there are many more, but on closer observation ultimately there are only those two. When you realize whether your actions are from love or power, you can make better choices.

One dictionary I Googled defines power as *the ability to do or act; capability of doing or accomplishing something.* Your internal power to do, to create, to take actions to elevate your life in some fashion is absolutely fabulous. This is the positive aspect of power. But when you use power to control others, or to take away their freedom to choose, or use force to interfere in their life, *because of course you know better*, this is the negative aspect of power, which is "power over." I will refer only to the negative aspect of power going forward. And know this is the exact opposite of love.

When you distill any lesson from this Earth university, it is really all about love or power.

What do I mean when I use the word love? There are many definitions of love: romance, lust, affection, family, and on and on. Since this book is about miracles, karma, and reincarnation, my definition of love is different, directing your focus to grow towards the highest interpretation. I want you to understand and relate to yourself as Soul and realize everything in life is teaching you some aspect of love or power. While you go about your daily life with all its many complexities, aspects, and adventures, Spirit is trying to reach the heart of your true self - Soul - helping you become a greater vehicle of Divine Love.

So here goes. Love - Divine Love - is always uplifting to you and others. This doesn't mean you become a doormat or a martyr sacrificing yourself. It does mean you treat yourself with respect, and keep healthy boundaries with yourself and others. But really, the elevated way of understanding love is defined this way by Harold Klemp from his book, *How the Inner Master Works*, "Perhaps then-as-now too few people knew how to love themselves. I'm not talking about loving the little self the egotistical side, the selfless the greedy side. I am talking about loving that part of yourself that is divine. Love that part of yourself that is divine, because that is Soul, and you are Soul."

If you are Soul, then others are Soul, too. If you conduct yourself with this kind of respect, you can learn to love yourself more deeply and treat all other people with the same kind of deference. You may not want to

CHAPTER FIVE

socially interact with all or any of them, and that is absolutely ok, but you do give them courtesy and space to live *their* lives.

I must admit, I am not always successful at this, but I work at sending detached Divine Love to strangers or people that are not in my circle of family or close friends. Inwardly I wish them well. This is agape.

In my opinion agape is the highest level of love to offer. It's given without any expectations of receiving anything in return. Offering agape is a **decision** to spread detached Divine Love in any circumstance. In my opinion, it is not possible to give warm love to everyone. Warm love is given to family, close friends, and romantic partners that are capable of reciprocity. But goodwill or detached love, now that, we can give to everyone.

Notice the bold word, **decision**.

Let's take a deeper dive into how this may look in your life.

When I met my husband Mark, I was healing from my second divorce. What happens to fracture most relationships is the subtle creeping of power that is manifested by the need to control. It's very much like the title of the long running off Broadway musical, *I love you, you're perfect, now change!*

We meet someone, fall in love and before long we are trying to change them.

My clear example is when I saw Mark drinking Mountain Dew for his morning beverage, I remember thinking to myself, Mountain Dew, for goodness' sake. Let me tell you, I had to mightily rein in my inner, chattering thoughts that were dissing his beverage preference. My itty, bitty internal voice committee was really quite agitated. I *knew* what was best for his health, I *knew* that Mountain Dew wasn't good for him, and on and on.

Luckily for Mark and our relationship, I stopped trying to control him. Control is an aspect of power. At that time in my life, I started to recognize and perceive the subtle brush strokes of power though I wanted to live and flourish in love as much as possible. I gave Mark space to make his own choices, and I worked inwardly to let go of my internal attachment that he should do things my way.

Power can infiltrate an individual's life in very subtle and almost sneaky ways. My story about Mark and my struggle with Mountain Dew is a simple example of just how tricky and how easily you can slip into the consciousness of power.

Another example of this would be, telling someone they must go to your doctor because your doctor is the best and getting upset or judgmental if they choose their own path of healing.

Judging someone for their personal choices is an aspect of power. Yes, maybe your doctor really could help them better and maybe you know that they are sabotaging their health, but on the playing field of Soul, they are in charge of the direction of their life and development, even if they choose a course of hardship. At times diffi-

CHAPTER FIVE

culties are karmic lessons and sometimes those troubles are helping that Soul grow, and this might be the fastest route.

An analogy would be, you seeing a monarch butterfly struggling to get out of its cocoon. You, coming from a good place, want to help the butterfly. But by your assisting the butterfly out of its cocoon, it had no struggle. Consequently its wings come out misshapen. A monarch butterfly actually needs the hard struggle of getting out of its cocoon to create its beautiful wings. Many people's misfortunes and problems are the shaping process they need spiritually, whether we or they know this consciously or not.

You are probably like most people and want to help others. The desire to control someone can arise when you are really trying to help. I have found it extremely difficult to let the people I love make what I perceive as a mistake. The way I now approach this is if I think I have an idea of what can help someone, I suggest *my* idea maybe twice and then drop *my* need for whether they adopt my suggestion. This letting go is especially hard when you know from experience that if they do what you recommend they will get better results. What you don't know is the X Factor, that as Soul they may need to go through problems or difficulties to develop. Keep in mind, it's not only about this one lifetime, but what this lifetime of choices will bring to an individual Soul going forward, in this life and in future lives.

When we think of a person who uses power to control, we often think of authoritarian world leaders, con men, angry mobs, or people who are violent. In these scenarios it is easier to spot the negative use of power and control. It's not so easy to spot within the confines of your own thinking or your actions and interactions with family and loved ones.

So what does this have to do with miracles, karma, or reincarnation?

Let's go back to my Mountain Dew meltdown. This time, let's see what might have happened if I continued to articulate my "concern" over the nefarious beverage choice. I imagine it would probably go something like this. "Mark, you know drinking Mountain Dew is terrible for you, right?" He would probably disagree, and tell me he liked the stuff, and continue drinking his Mountain Dew.

A few days later the inner urge to confront him would surface within me on what I now viewed as egregious behavior. Again, more strongly this time, I voiced my "worry" for his health, but inwardly, truth be told, I was irritated he would not listen to my sage advice and I also was attached to my perspective about Mountain Dew.

Time goes on, more Mountain Dew gets drunk, and I am at my wit's end. I love that man, and I care for him, but for goodness' sake, he is not listening to me. Me, who I have now deemed, the "All Knowing One."

Mark, rightly so, was getting really sick of my pushing him to do things my way. We would get into a fight or a few fights and love was put on the back burner. Understand that by trying to control Mark, I have just created some negative karma. Probably not the kind that sinks ships, but still it's on the side of power, not love.

Imagine what my future karma could look like. Maybe, I would be reborn working for Mountain Dew or be someone that drinks it and has someone trying to control *my* drinking it, all because of my need to control Mark.

Irony aside, karma is not about punishment, it is a tool to educate each Soul to take true, total responsibility for all actions and ultimately to learn to have a greater capacity to love all of life, yourself included. Part of the lesson of learning to love all of life is to give others their space to make their own mistakes and choices.

So back to the miracle part. The true miracle that happened to me in the Mountain Dew example is I learned to give Mark room and space to be himself. By giving Mark freedom to make is own choices, I came from love and, hence, created more love in our relationship simply by letting go of my need to control. A little miracle, but a miracle nonetheless, especially since I came from two failed marriages.

Yes, some of this story may seem trite, but the essence of non-interference and karma holds true. I hope you understand just how easy it is to come from power rather than love. Think of, all the little power struggles you may experienced over how to do housework, finances, socializing, etc. Maintaining your personal boundaries is absolutely correct and necessary and different than trying to control another person. Your personal boundaries are about taking care of you, not someone else.

If you have children, it's a different story. As a good parent your job is to protect, nurture, and teach your little ones how to be good adults. While they are developing and maturing you may have to enforce rules with them and educate them for their highest good, but what they then choose to do when they reach adulthood is totally in their hands.

The more profound aspect of karma is the process of facing ourselves, our choices of thoughts, and our actions. You cannot run away from or hide from karma. But you can soften the process through spiritual exercises and through understanding and integrating what you learn about any particular situation and then implementing your knowledge in your actions. I did exactly that when I realized I was trying to control my husband's choice of Mountain Dew. Through my decision not to control, I gained some wisdom and perspective on the many facets of power.

How to use daily living to evolve spiritually.

When I mention spiritual growth, I notice many people back away from the subject. For many individuals, the idea of spiritual growth invokes restrictive or negative connotations of God or Spirit. Maybe through reading or experience, they came to understand spiritual growth as something gained by adopting a dogmatic or judgmental belief system. Also throughout history, innumerable men and women have used religion to control and punish others and create selfish gains. If this is your only exposure to what spiritual life is like, I understand your hesitancy to open your heart to spiritual

CHAPTER FIVE

living.

Your life is a spiritual journey whether you are conscious of it or not, because Spirit permeates all of existence. There is no separation from Spirit, just degrees of your awareness of Spirit. You do not need traditional religion to grow on your path. My personal journey has taken me on multiple paths, some traditional and others not so much. I want you to know whatever path or no path you are on is absolutely ok. You are as unique as I am, and your adventure and avenue of spiritual growth will be particular to your individual consciousness.

Here's a snapshot of my spiritual pilgrimage. I was raised, as I said earlier, as a Catholic. For many years I was very devout. I read about the Catholic saints and admired their pious lives. But as I got older, the Catholic Church seemed very unapproachable and I couldn't relate to its doctrines. They just didn't resonate with what was in my heart.

Around the time I left home at 15 I also left the Catholic Church, still seeking the next step in my personal path to the Divine. Since to me the Catholic Church was very dogmatic, my next phase of evolution in the school of the Spirit was to become agnostic. No formal path, but I left the door open to see if there was really a God.

I read a lot of esoteric and metaphysical books as a young adult. Through this doorway of learning, I came to deeply feel and believe there is a Divine presence that permeates all of existence. I realized this because of my own efforts, not because an authority figure told me I had to believe in a certain way.

I held onto being agnostic until my mid-twenties when I met my first husband. By this time I was having inner nudges to have a spiritual practice. A spiritual practice for me means a discipline that strengths you, like daily meditation or contemplation. It's the spiritual mirror of physical exercise. You don't have to do daily workouts for your body if you don't want to, and you will get the results from those actions. But if you do something daily to strengthen your body, the physical part of you will benefit. The same is true with incorporating a daily spiritual exercise, like contemplation, meditation, or prayer.

For a couple of years I would intermittently try quiet meditation (the kind where you work at stilling your thoughts) and all I got were great naps! So when my first husband introduced me to a form of Buddhism that used mantras spoken out loud, I took to it immediately. In this practice, I repeated aloud a mantra for about 30 minutes a day. I liked it and realized I could stay awake for that!

The dictionary defines a mantra as *a word or sound repeated to aid concentration in meditation.* I want to add my own awareness to what a mantra means. A mantra is an internal tuning fork for your inner awareness as Soul. It helps lift your consciousness above the downward pull, negativity, and limiting energy of this physical reality. Simply put, it is food for your Soul! That spiritual nourishment feeds every part of you.

By repeating my mantra daily, I started to blossom on every level, I was feeling happier and more stable.

CHAPTER FIVE

I also was learning discipline. This was different than quiet mediations. It's akin to reading about exercise and actually doing the exercise. I got out of my mental rumination and into action.

I stayed with this form of Buddhism for about eight years. Though I was very earnest in my practice, it took me as far as I could go. I still had nagging questions regarding what happens after the body dies, and I wanted to know about the transcendental aspects of love. This practice could not answer my questions, and I also had continual, inner stirrings of needing more. I didn't quite know what the more was, but as I look back I had what I called Soul's discontent. The inner push to go forward spiritually.

Consequently, I asked inwardly of the Universe, God, or Spirit for a new practice. I absolutely learned through my time as a Buddhist the power of daily spiritual connecting. I waited and kept my heart open, knowing the right vehicle existed for me.

One day I went to the tiny, little bookcase in my apartment to look for a book, and I found a book on Eckankar, which is a spiritual path based in Divine Love and spiritual freedom. I had no earthly understanding of how that book got on my shelf. This bookcase was very small, and I had foraged through it many times in search of a good read. Yet here was this book. I picked it up and started to chant a word from one of its pages. That mantra took me to a place of peace faster than anything I had experienced as a Buddhist. I had found my next step! Think about it: I had that bookcase my whole adult life, I never saw that volume before, and I didn't know how it got there. Yet the book, my next step, my personal direction of inner growth, was right there. For me, it was another miracle (or as my husband so cheerfully says, a "woo, woo" moment).

You may be saying to yourself "Now, well, that is all well and good for you, but I have real problems in daily life and reciting mantras or doing spiritual exercises isn't going to help solve my real problems." I beg to differ, please hear me out. Tapping into and honing your spiritual senses help you in every way and on every level of your being for the big and small issues that arise in your life. Here are other examples from my own life.

How connecting daily to the Divine can help your daily life.

Have you ever started on a big change in your life, like buying or selling a house or starting a business, or wondered if I should go to school or take a different career path? When you align yourself more closely to Spirit you will be given guidance through dreams, inner nudges, or intuition for your highest good.

For example, years ago I was contemplating moving my office from an office park rental to buying a free standing house in a subdivision to work out of. This way of working with clients would be different, and I was very apprehensive about losing my living. I didn't know if my clients would like coming to a house which I was not actually going to be living in. I also worried that the neighbors might complain; and then I would be stuck with a big purchase and problems if things didn't

CHAPTER FIVE

run smoothly.

I initially planned to look for a house after my lease was up the next year. Well, silly me, I went a year early to investigate what was available. And, of course, I found the perfect little ranch on a cul-de-sac in the exact neighborhood I wanted, five minutes from where I was living and in my price range.

At that time houses were selling fast so I put in my offer, even though I still had a year to go on my lease. The sellers accepted my offer because mine was first, even though many other offers came in after mine and some were higher.

Now I really started to panic. About that time, outside my window at my present office, an impressively, big hawk sat on a tree branch for hours looking into my window at me. Hawks were and are an important symbol for me to inwardly take notice of the events in my life.

This went on for about a week. I began to realize I was getting a message from Spirit, though I wasn't clear yet what the meaning was. Spirit speaks to us in any way we will listen.

Regardless of my knowing I was receiving a Spiritual message, I was still staying up at night worried about whether I had bought the house too quickly. I also still had that lease commitment on my office space for another year.

About two weeks after I put the contract on the house, a good friend had a dream about me. She told me that she saw a small ranch house that was mine. In the front yard was a huge pile of pine straw and with very large hawk sitting on it. She told me that the dream conveyed a feeling of abundance.

I had never told my friend that the house I put the contract on was a ranch, and I had never mentioned the address. The street the house was located on was Soft Pine Trail! Spirit used her to communicate to me that all would be fine and good. After that I relaxed. I easily found reliable renters to cover my lease and I ended up using that house as my office for over 20 years. And by the way, my clients loved coming to a warm house atmosphere instead of being in an office environment.

Inner nudges are often Spirit's way of communicating. You can tell if it is from the Divine if the nudge is not indicating any way to harm anyone or anything.

More Nudges.

One time sitting at a stop light, I got a very strong inner guidance from Spirit. I was waiting for the light to turn green. I would be the first car to go through. The light turned green, and on the other road there was no sign of any cars. Inwardly, I heard a strong, authoritative voice telling me to stay, not go. I did stay put, and out of nowhere a car came screaming through the red light. If I had gone when the light changed, I would have been hit broadside by the speeding car. I sat there in amazement, and from my heart I expressed deep gratitude. Another miracle!

Have you ever had the experience where someone

CHAPTER FIVE

you trust is asking you to do something, but you "get a feeling" something is not right? This happened to me. It was another concrete way the Divine helped me. This time, I avoided a bad financial situation.

About 25 years ago a trusted associate of mine, whom I will call Hal, came to me with a business opportunity. I had known him for many years. He was a man of integrity and very honest. But I got this funny feeling in the pit of my stomach about the venture. The investment was a lot of money for me at a time when I couldn't afford to lose any.

Soon after, while I was doing my internal debate, a client causally mentioned something about the company Hal wanted me to invest in. What the client said was not flattering.

I shook off the comment because I knew Hal better than I knew the client. In my daily spiritual exercise I asked again to be led for my highest good regarding this venture.

Three days later another client also "just mentioned" something about the company telling me it seemed off. Again, I blew off the comment because of the relationship I had with Hal. Fervently, every day I kept asking for guidance and a sign of what to do. The deadline to invest was approaching, and I had to make a decision.

Well, lo and behold, a third client in that same week, again out of the blue, started telling me how unethical this company was and not to trust them. None of these clients knew I was thinking about investing in the company. They were just blowing off steam in their sessions.

After three clients said the same thing, the message finally got through to me. I told my friend Hal I wasn't going to invest, but I wished him much success.

Fast forward, two years later: I ran into Hal and I asked him about the company he wanted me to invest in. It turned out that he lost all the money he put into the company because it was unethical in its ways of doing business.

I realized I had been guided by Spirit for my highest good. I didn't need to go through the experience of losing money at this juncture to help me develop spiritually. Hal, also Soul, for whatever reason, had his experience to learn what he needed on his personal journey.

The more you elevate your consciousness, the easier it is to pick up subtle (and in my case, not so subtle) nudges from the Divine to help you.

How I changed my negative relationship karma.

Another huge example of working inwardly to effect positive change in my life came after my second divorce.

Throughout my life, my romantic relationships had been either abusive or with men who didn't show up to participate until I met my present husband, Mark. Now I tease Mark that I "created" him. Let me explain.

After my second divorce, (I was in my late thirties by this time), I took a hard look at myself and my history with men and relationships. I could have very

CHAPTER FIVE

easily slipped into the traps many men and women believe. They tell themselves that there are no good men out there, or all women are out for themselves, or that they are always going to get hurt. On and on, with the negative beliefs and self-talk about the opposite sex and relationships, Yada, yada, yada.

Karmic patterns in your life can show up as a persistent repetition of something good or something negative. (My bulimia was, I believe, a karmic pattern, because the only way I healed it was through working with a spiritual exercise.) I try to live in earnest from the law of cause and effect that pervades all of life. So after my second divorce I took a very, long, hard look at me. I saw a karmic pattern in my life: not just one bad relationship, but many.

I was adamantly determined to end my cycle of bad or so-so relationships. Coincidentally, that year Eckankar was having a spiritual seminar over July fourth weekend in Minneapolis. People from all over the world were coming to take workshops, meet friends, and get spiritually replenished. I really, really needed that, so off I went.

I spotted a workshop titled "Spiritual Goal Setting" that was teaching how to integrate any goal you may have for your higher good, and in the process, evolve more consciously as a vehicle of Spirit. What I learned through that class absolutely touched the core of my being. I remember to this day what I said internally. It has been the most powerful statement I have ever said to myself: **Let me face whatever I need to face within**

myself that is keeping me from a longterm, loving, and joyful romantic relationship.

This was a weighty and significant commitment I gave to myself and to Spirit. I realized whether I found this relationship in this lifetime or not, by doing the internal spiritual work on myself, I would create a higher quality of life.

When you live knowing you create and have created all that is in your life it can be exhilarating. No more victimhood, just opportunities. If you use your life to develop your experiences with expanded awareness, you become the captain of your life travels.

I went home back to Atlanta, and determined to start an inner development course of facing myself. Whether I got a great romantic relationship or not, I now was on a higher road of transformation.

Every day I did a spiritual exercise, starting with singing the HU, followed by visualizing my inner self accepting love from a man who was for my foremost good. I took considerable care observe to how I felt in my body and what thoughts and feelings arose when I focused on accepting love.

What surfaced led me to heal parts of my childhood, change limiting beliefs I didn't realize I even still had, and work on releasing anger and fears from my past. I refused to gloss over anything that came up for me to face.

Over the weeks and, yes, months of this inner work, I noticed my thoughts were settling down, becoming more neutral or positive. My emotions of anger and fear were also lessening.

For anything to be created in this physical existence there has to be two components: inner change and outer action. So my everyday commitment to my inner work was also coupled with my going out and meeting men. I joined a phone dating service (this was before dating apps or the internet). At least once a week I met a guy for coffee. Through this process I actually got to know myself better and realized what I truly wanted in a relationship. I called this process my dating school.

I did the "one date, coffee date," for months, and I never got discouraged. I recognized this was my way of knowing myself on a deeper platform. Through these coffee dates, I met some wonderful people, but I didn't make a romantic connection with any of them. I kept looking at my method of dating as a way to grow spiritually. At the time, I was healing aspects of my past that interfered with my having a healthy romantic relationship. I was learning to love and value myself and know what I truly wanted and needed in a relationship.

After a few months, I had a dream that revealed my karma regarding bad relationships was almost gone. All the internal spiritual work I was doing was starting to pay off. I still did my spiritual exercises every morning and continued the dating interview process.

Remember, I said I lived in Atlanta Georgia? For those of you who are unfamiliar with Atlanta and its traffic let me paint you a picture. Atlanta has over six million people, and very little public transportation so almost everyone drives. The expressways are six to eight lanes across, and most of the day there is crushing traffic.

I was driving one day on a fun-filled expressway, just kind of in my own little world, focused on maneuvering among all the trucks and endless cars. I soon became aware of two cars in front of me that were next to each other. The car on the left had a Life Chiropractic College bumper sticker. The car next to it on the right had a Canadian flag bumper sticker. Now, dear reader, my first husband went to Life Chiropractic College, and my second husband was a Canadian.

At this juncture of the expressway you could go straight or turn to the left. I always intended to turn to the left. The two cars with the bumper stickers went straight and stayed together.

This is what I call a waking dream. The Divine was telling me my karma with my two ex-husbands was now over. Think. What is the probability in a traffic-filled place like Atlanta that two cars with those exact stickers would be in front of my car long enough for me to notice and then drive in a different direction? There are no accidents in life. Spirit is always talking to us, just sometimes more overtly than other times.

I do love puns, and I believe Spirit has a sense of humor and delivers messages that are unique to each person, each Soul. In my waking dream the cars were symbolic of my ex-husbands and their cars driving away in a different path showed my "carma" (karma) with them was over. I was so excited to see this little

CHAPTER FIVE

miracle, it was an affirmation and waking dream that I was healing.

After that, I continued doing my regular spiritual exercises and went to the get-to-know-you coffees. I then had several dreams that I was going to meet a man soon who would be very important in my life. (Dreams and waking dreams are another way Spirit communicates to us. I devote more time to this later, but know your life can become much smoother if you become aware of your dreams and waking dreams and what they are trying to convey.)

A few months later I had my first date with Mark. It was on the fourth of July *exactly one year to the day* after I inwardly made the commitment to face whatever I needed to face within myself to have a joyful, loving, and uplifting relationship. We married seven years later on the fourth of July, and have been happily married for over twenty years. I hope my stories illustrates that a path of connecting to Spirit can help you heal old issues and guide you to a better life right here, right now.

Personal Notes

6

Dreams, Their Deeper Purpose, and How to Interpret Them

The subject of dreams is incredibly fascinating, and what they can teach you is limitless. People have been delving into the meaning and purpose of dreams, I believe, since humans developed conscious awareness.

What, exactly, is a dream? Some believe they are our unconscious mind unloading the day's events or trying to process something that is bothering us. Nightmares are common for little children, and some adults have them. What are they trying to convey?

I am personally of the opinion our night time dreams are much more profound and esoteric than simply the mind sloughing off of the daily events or processing childhood issues, though dreams certainly can do that. More importantly, dreaming is the way Soul – which, remember, is your true self – continues to explore life and its multiple planes of existence in this physical reality and beyond. These inner dimensions I am referring to are the worlds of Spirit or the different levels of heaven.

You may be thinking you just want to know what dreaming about cats means. Or why you always dream about Italy. We'll get how to interpret your dreams and much more, but first I want to give you an overview and look at the wisdom and profundity of dreams. This is to help you delve into a deeper comprehension that dreaming is really an integral part of the spiritual experience. I want to whet your appetite to explore the full scope of the dream world.

Types of dreams.

There are different types of dreams: Ones about past lives, waking dreams, prophetic dreams, lucid dreams (which I call Soul Travel) and recurring dreams are the kinds most people experience. Dreams also help you communicate to other people or Souls when the need arises. When you take the time to decipher and understand the symbols in your night time dream, it is easier to make sense of them.

If you are not having a true lucid Soul travel experience, then more than likely you remember your dreams in symbols. Your job is to learn your dream language. No one, not any book or Google search, can interpret your dreams for you. Your lifetimes of unique experiences provide distinctive and individualized meanings to whatever you dream.

To develop your own understanding of what the objects in your dreams mean to you, start off by listing a couple of objects you recall from dreams and ask yourself, "What does this symbol mean to me?" For example, I love cats. They are my symbol for love. Someone

CHAPTER SIX

who hates cats and dreams about them will not give cats the same symbolism I do.

When I Googled the most frequent dream subjects, this is what came up:

1: Water Dreams

2: Vehicles (cars or vans)

3: Being trapped somewhere

4: Teeth falling out or wobbling

5: Babies or having children

6: Animals (all animals)

7: Being chased by something

8: Death or dying

Here are some possibilities for meanings:

Water can symbolize Spirit, emotions, or the subconscious. Vehicles can symbolize yourself or your state of consciousness. Being trapped might mean you are stuck in some way or, depending on the context of the dream, maybe a past life. Teeth falling out could mean repressed anger. When I dream of babies or having children, I look to my inner child or childhood. Animals can represent emotions or a spiritual totem. Being chased by someone or something can mean you are not facing something on some level or feel threatened in some way. Dreams of death might mean rebirth or facing the fear of the death of the physical body.

You may have other associations. Feel free to use Google or any other resource to stimulate some ideas, but be sure the meaning resonates with you.

When you have a dream and you want to comprehend it, start by asking yourself what aspects of the dream have meaning for you right now. Avoid saying, "I don't know." You close off your inner guidance when you say I don't know. By being your own detective, you harness your intuition, the part of you that is connected to yourself as Soul. There is *always* a part of you that knows. A way to help yourself perceive the answer is to ask, "What if I did know?" Then listen to what emerges.

I consistently give my clients dream suggestions in the hypnotic MP3's I make for them. When they come back to their session and report their dreams, I ask, "What do you think this means to you?" At first, almost all of my clients say "I don't know." Then by taking the time and asking questions (as if you did know) invariably an answer surfaces. When you do this, you are developing a process to understand yourself more consciously and at a deeper level.

Trust your intuition. Part of you is cognizant of the meaning of your dream. Listen to your body. Many times when you are ruminating on an answer your heart area or stomach will become lighter, or you may experience an "ah ha" moment.

If dream work interests you, keep a journal by your bed. Write down anything you remember. Review what you have written once a week, and look at the dream from the viewpoint of your present situation. This is a

CHAPTER SIX

wonderful place to start.

Dreams can help your daily life.

Let me give you a personal example. Once I dreamed several men were trying to break into my house. I staved them off, but I was still scared in the dream. After I woke up, I wrote down what I remembered of the dream and analyzed it, relating the symbology to what was going on in my life.

The men signified threats, and I protected myself in the dream by keeping them out of my house which represented myself. At that time I was learning about boundaries. This dream confirmed for me to keep my boundaries strong, even if I still was not comfortable communicating my boundaries to others or following through with healthy ones.

Another time I was going to oil painting classes and felt very inferior to the other art students. My teacher was and is an amazing artist and fabulous instructor. A couple of months after I started lessons I dreamed I was attracted to my art teacher. Even in the dream I recall saying to myself, "I am not attracted to him, and I am married." I dutifully wrote down my dream in the morning, including my feelings. Frankly, I was a little disturbed by the dream so I asked a close friend if she had any insight. She immediately picked up that I subconsciously wanted to assimilate and absorb some of my art teacher's ability. As soon as she said that, I had the "ah, ha" moment, and her explanation felt totally right.

I analyze each dream in relation to my daily life and

ask myself what am I trying to learn, or what is Spirit trying to teach me. I always stay true to my inner knowing or intuition of what my symbols are trying to convey.

When you work with your dreams as part of your connection to the Divine, you will never be led to do something to hurt others or yourself. Always look at your dreams from a positive viewpoint, even if they are a little disturbing or on first blush seem negative. The learning may happen on any level, emotionally, mentally, physically or spiritually. Keep in mind dreams are in your life to help you.

For example, when I first came onto the path of Eckankar after being a Buddhist, I had many dreams of tornadoes. When I took this symbol into my daily contemplation, I began to realize I was processing deep anger and facing beliefs about death. Because I stayed true to my intuition, I knew and understood the dream wasn't preparing me to encounter a tornado. I kept asking myself, what then would this big wind represent? I was experiencing a lot of anger at that period of my life, and Eckankar taught me much about what happens after the death of the body. (I never got any understanding of life after death through my Buddhist practice. It was one of the reasons I left.) When these two realizations came to the forefront of my consciousness, I had the inner sense that the dream was trying to help me process and release my anger more gently through dreaming and assist in liberating me from some of my fear of death.

CHAPTER SIX

Prophetic Dreams.

Precognition or prophetic dreams are sent by Spirit to help you or prepare you for something that may be burdensome or overwhelming coming your way. They can be difficult to recognize. Sometimes you may get a knowing, like an inner feeling, that this is a possible future that may manifest. Other times you may not recognize what the dream means until you read it in your dream journal at a later date. Then you understand that, indeed, this dream was telling you your future.

One of my prophetic dreams was right before I divorced my first husband. I saw our house collapse, but I was ok. At the time I didn't know what the dream was telling me. A few months later when we started divorce proceedings, I still didn't understand that Spirit was telling me my future. I didn't get the symbology until I was married for the second time, and I had a very similar dream of my house imploding. In the second dream I was told I had insurance, which I interpreted to mean that I would come through the divorce with a higher consciousness.

I really didn't want to believe I would be going through yet another divorce, so I asked my same friend who gave me advice on the dream about my art teacher to help me understand this dream. I confided I was concerned about going through another divorce. She very confidently said, "No, I don't think that is what the dream meant."

Sadly, deep in my heart I knew I was headed for another divorce, regardless of how sure my friend was or how much I really didn't want another divorce. About six months after I had this dream, my second husband and I divorced. Always know you are the ultimate authority of your dream interpretation.

Keep in mind that we all possess free will, and even if you have a precognition dream it is still only a "possible" future. Your now is always creating, based on your actions, reactions, and your state of consciousness.

I had another very direct dream of prophecy right before I wrote my first book. Writing had never been a habit or a hobby of mine, even as a little girl or younger woman. I never planned on writing a book when I had this incredibly, vivid dream. That night in my dream a voice told me I would be writing books to help teach people more elevated ways of living and perceiving existence. I was extremely confused and concerned when I heard this in the dream, but I *knew* it would come to be. The last thing I remember was me screaming back to the voice, "But I can't spell!" End of dream.

Now, I wondered, what was I going to do with this information? Months went by. I put the dream in the back of my mind and focused on my work and daily life. Then I got an inner nudge to use my computer for daily journaling of my dreams. Bang! This opened up the floodgates for Spirit to use me a vehicle to disseminate information through writing a book. I literally heard words pour through me as a stream of consciousness. Very quickly the format came into my mind, and I found my fabulous editor, Phyllis. Who without her expertise I know I could never have accomplished writing that book. I got all the help I needed, and being completely honest I had no idea what I was doing, I was just compelled to write.

My first book, You Are Soul, helped me grow in consciousness through the writing process, and I have been told by countless individuals that they were helped by reading it. I believe if I hadn't had such a lucid, striking, and prophetic dream, I wouldn't have had the impetus or courage to go through with creating my first book.

Dreams can connect Soul to Soul.

Another kind of divination dream can be when people connect at night when they sleep. Keep in mind you are Soul, and so are other people. At night when we sleep we are learning, and sometimes we connect with each other for a purpose.

Such was the case with my dear friend Joy. One night she had a crystal clear dream that her sister was in a car accident. She woke up several times in the night and when she went back to sleep, she would find herself right back in this compelling and realistic dream.

Miles away, in another state, a friend of Joy's was wondering whether to confide to her about a disturbing situation that she was experiencing. That night the friend focused on what was the right thing to do. In the morning she decided to bring Joy into her confidence.

First thing in the morning Joy's friend called her and shared what was bothering her. Immediately Joy comprehended that this was what her dream was about. She *knew* this without a doubt. This dream softened the blow of the disconcerting news Joy received from her friend. (Just to make sure, Joy called her biological sister and found out she was fine.)

There is always a higher spiritual reason for the dreams we receive. They are there to help us, not to benefit our ego.

Communication with Souls in animal form.

Soul can take on the body of an animal. This doesn't mean the animal is less than or that being in human form is higher or better. It means that particular Soul needs that experience for its development. Here are two examples of dream communication with my cats Zippity and Foot.

My cat Zippity was this big, gray sweetie, and even though she was over 14 pounds she had this very distinctive tiny, high pitched mew. I would rub her tummy every morning and play with her in a gentle way to match her spirit, but for a couple of months I had gotten out of the habit of playing with her.

One day I noticed she was starting to lick her fur off. As any cat owner knows, when cats do this it is usually because something is bothering them. The trick is to find out what it is. Inwardly I kept asking Spirit to assist me in helping Zippity and find out why she was pulling out her fur. Quite soon after I started to focus from my heart in asking Spirit for help, I had a dream. In the dream Zippity talked to me in English but with an extremely high voice, much like her mew.

She told me that she was sad because I had stopped

CHAPTER SIX

playing with her in the mornings. I was taken aback by what she said. I told her in the dream that I was so sorry and that I would play with her every morning from now on just like I used to do, so please stop licking off your fur. Through our communication in the dream, love was flowing between us again and Zippity knew I would keep my word to play with her from now on.

In the morning I reconfirmed to her that I would play with her every morning and that I was very sorry for not keeping up with it. From that day on she never pulled out her fur again, and I kept my word of playing with her in the mornings.

Life, the Divine, is always communicating to us. Dreams are a major way you can learn about life and what Spirit is trying to teach or convey.

My dear cat Foot had extra toes on each paw, and they resembled feet, hence the name Foot. We shared our lives for 17 years. She was a very developed Soul. I know she came into my life to help me during some of my toughest years. She was always there to give me comfort and solace. At night I remember us traveling the inner planes together. We had an exceptionally powerful love bond.

Sadly her physical life was coming to an end. She had liver cancer and I had to make the tough decision to end her suffering. I went with her to the vet in tears. But through the whole procedure I sang HU silently, and by singing HU I put that dear Soul into the hands of the Holy Spirit.

Needless to say, afterward I was devastated, but I had to continue to work and see clients. I thought since Foot and I had shared so many night time adventures together I would see her again in my dreams, but this wasn't happening and I didn't understand why.

About three weeks after her passing, I was working with a client. I always ask my clients if they have had any dreams and this particular one never had any to report, until that day.

She reported that yes, indeed, she did have a dream, and it was about me. In the dream she saw me as half cat and half human, and I smiled and said I was happy. As I listened to her relate her dream, I started to have chills. I asked her what color the cat part was and she said, "black and white." Foot was black and white!

Soul, which had the life as Foot, communicated to me through my client. The dream my client related told me helped me realize that Foot was happy, and that she would be reincarnating as a human in her next life.

I understood, then, that my grief had stopped the communication between us. But Foot had found a way to reach me because of her love for me, and she let me know she was really happy.

Waking dreams.

Spirit can also communicate to you through daily occurrences. You can recognize the message because something someone says or a situation really speaks to you.

CHAPTER SIX

My friend Stacie had a particularly dynamic waking dream that saved her baby son. She was in the hospital after the birth of her second child, a boy, and she was sharing the room with another new mom.

The other woman's doctor came in to give the other mom instructions. Stacie couldn't help but overhear their conversation. Upon hearing the doctor's first two instructions, Stacie mentally said to herself, "I know that." The third instruction by the doctor was specific and quite firm. He said, "If the baby's temperature ever goes over 100 bring him to the hospital immediately." He was warning the other mother that this could be a symptom of something extremely serious. My friend recalled thinking, well, I don't know that, and she mentally filed away that bit of information.

A week or two later Stacie was breastfeeding her son, and he felt warm. She took his temperature. It was 100.1. She remembered what the doctor said to the other woman and she immediately had her husband rush their son to the hospital while she stayed home with their toddler.

Someone else may have balked at taking their child to the hospital because it was one tenth over the 100 degree mark, but Stacie was insistent.

At the hospital the baby was immediately started on antibiotics before they took any tests. One of the fears for newborns with temperatures over a 100 is bacterial meningitis, which spreads incredibly fast and is often fatal in infants.

The pediatrician who just "happened" to be on call was the same doctor who told the other new mother about getting her baby to the hospital if the baby's fever was above 100.

The test came back positive for bacterial meningitis, but because Stacie and her husband acted so quickly and the hospital staff started the baby on antibiotics right away he lived and is now a strapping young man. What happened to Stacie was indeed a miracle!

Spirit spoke to Stacie through that pediatrician. Because of her awareness, she heeded the warning and acted on it. This is a powerful example of a waking dream.

Be assured you are never alone, and you are getting guidance all the time. Learn to trust your intuition and inner nudges. Think back to the different occurrences in your life when you got an inner nudge that helped you avoid something negative or prepared you for a change of some kind. The more you listen, the stronger your intuition becomes.

My powerful waking dream.

Waking dreams can be messengers of hope and learning. A few years back I was dealing with groin pain, which inhibited my inability to walk any distance. I am a fairly active person. I do yoga and Pilates, play golf, and walk for exercise. My normal activity level was doing one of those things daily, until the groin issue interfered with my walking. It got to a point that even after a gentle walk I was in pain.

I was totally flummoxed. I couldn't figure out what

CHAPTER SIX

was going on. I went to my chiropractor and massage therapist, and I applied cold packs, but nothing seemed to help. What really sent me down a depressed "rabbit hole" was when my husband and I had to cancel a vacation we had planned because it involved a lot of walking, which at that time I couldn't do.

I took this problem into my daily spiritual exercises asking for help and answers. I also requested to learn from this experience. Nothing came up directly in my contemplation, but a few days later Spirit answered me in a wonderfully compelling and creative way.

Once a month I lead a HU song contemplation for 20 to 30 minutes at the local senior center. Singing the HU is followed by open discussion. On this particular day, two women came, and after the HU we all had a brief chat then one of them left. The remaining lady and I had a lengthy conversation. I found out her name was also Marian and she spelled it just like I do. (We Marians don't find too many of us around.) As we continued to talk I found out her middle name was the same as mine, and she was born in the same year I was. We were both named Marian for the same reason. Both of us were raised Catholic. (The year we were born, in the Catholic religion, was called the Marian year.) Her husband was named Mark and had been born in Boston, just like my husband!

As she was talking and the similarities kept piling up, my inner awareness told me that our meeting and sharing was not a coincidence.

As she was just about to leave, she said something

totally off topic. She basically blurted out that she was glad to come today because she liked to stay active. She informed me that a few years ago she felt like she would never walk again due to an injury. Now, Marian said, "I can do anything I want to do, including dancing!"

Well, I just was dumbstruck! I was worried I would never be able to be as active or even take walks again. I heard her words and I knew they were for me from the Divine to hang in there. All would be ok.

Spirit sent me a powerful message in the only way I would listen. A sister Marian with the same issues, who got healed. Inwardly, I felt a huge weight lift from my heart. I still had pain, but I now knew there was an answer.

Fast forward a few months later. I consulted an orthopedist and found out my issues stemmed from my hip. The doctor told me eventually I may need a hip replacement if I choose that route, but afterward I would be able to do all the varied activities I want. As I write this book I am out of pain, utilizing many alternative remedies. For now they are working, and I am as active as I want to be. If in the future if I need a hip replacement, I know I will heal from that and be able to do normal activities.

My waking dream put my fears to rest and helped me know all will be ok.

A lifesaving, waking dream.

Stacie had another life changing waking dream when her children were in high school. For about sev-

CHAPTER SIX

en months she had endured debilitating migraine headaches. The pain, she said, was so bad that she was bedridden and couldn't do anything. No TV, no reading, just bed rest. Any light or noise created even more pain. On top of that, she couldn't keep food down and lost nearly 60 pounds.

She got very good at meditation and contemplation. Inwardly Stacie would "put it out there," as she phrased it, to the Universe or Spirit to help her. Over those months of agony, her friends gave her and her husband suggestions for doctors to consult and remedies to try. Nothing was working.

During this time they lived in Manhattan and had access to top medical care. Stacie and her husband saw the four top neurologists in New York City, but to no avail.

One day she had a short reprieve of her pain and Googled, "headache pain help New York City." Up came New York Headache Center and a doctor's name. She noticed the doctor was someone a friend had previously mentioned but she had not contacted him for some reason. Because she recalled the names matched, she called the clinic for an appointment with that doctor. She couldn't see that particular doctor for at least three months, but his new associate was free that day. Stacie was desperate so she took the appointment with the associate.

It just so happened that Stacie was the doctor's very first patient at the clinic. After Stacie described her symptoms, the doctor knew immediately what the problem was and diagnosed Hemi Crania Continua. Only

1% of the population has the condition, but this particular doctor had done her thesis on this condition. It was easily treatable by a unique aspirin compound called Indomethacin.

What is the likelihood that Stacie would have found this doctor at this time and would actually get in to see her? In my opinion, Stacie aligned herself inwardly to the directives of Spirit at the perfect time to get the help and healing she so needed. Yet another miracle!

Recurring dreams.

Dreams that you have over and over can mean different things. When I get dreams that repeat a theme, maybe with a slight variation, I examine what I am going through in my present daily life. I review my symbols, assign them meaning, and decipher the dream from that viewpoint.

Here are some of my recurring dreams and my interpretations of them.

Over a period of years, I dreamed about houses that were mine in the dream state. I was always renovating them. The houses symbolized my state of consciousness. The dreams were telling me I was working inwardly on some level. The renovations represented change and the upgrading of my consciousness and awareness.

Every time I dream about cats, since they are my symbol for love, I look for the meaning based on what is happening to the cats in the dreams. This gives me deeper insights to what I need to face and learn regarding love.

CHAPTER SIX

I have another recurring dream where I have either misplaced my car or it gets stolen. The first couple of times I dreamed about this I got very upset in the dream about my lost vehicle. After a while, I had so many of these dreams, that even in the dream state I would say, "Well, I know I will be ok." I knew when I was dreaming that I had insurance or that since it was a dream, my car in my physical life was ok. I believe these dreams are teaching me about detachment of the physical and to rely more deeply to my true nature as Soul.

When you are having a recurring dream, Spirit is trying to convey a message you may have overlooked or need to be aware of. Also, like my renovation dreams, the dreams reveal progress of some kind. Use your own interpretation of the symbols in the dreams to determine your individual message and understanding.

Lucid dreams.

Very simply, lucid or really, really, vivid dreams are more likely than not a true Soul Travel experience. As Soul, we travel at night in our dreams. The vividness or direct perception of that experience is usually garbled by our mind so we remember only bits and pieces of our journeys, but lucid dream experience is different, in that you recall your complete journey to the inner worlds unaltered in the morning.

Nightmares.

Nightmares can be an indication of past lives that were too painful. Your mind distorts the truth and gives you what you can handle. If you write them down and take the nightmare into contemplation, it can help you process the trauma from that past life.

Past life dreams.

When the subject of past lives comes up, many individuals fantasize about being royalty or a great historical figure, or they imagine some kind of life that pacifies their egos. In reality, we each have had hundreds, if not thousands, of lives, and most of them have been pretty mundane. Each life, though, from a spiritual perspective, teaches us in some way to accept more love and to give more love. The purpose of remembering a past life is to help you through a problem, to grow in awareness (Divine Love), or to work through karma.

You might be asking now, how do you know if the dream you had was about a past life? First look at the timing of the dream. For example, is the dream set in a distant time period such as the Middle Ages? What are the people in your dream wearing? Are they dressed in pioneer clothing for example? Do you sense in the dream that you are watching yourself? You also may be a different sex than you are in this lifetime. (You are Soul and as Soul you take on both male and female bodies. Soul just is.)

You will have a past life dream if it can help you in this lifetime in some way.

I will share with you my past life dream that helped me move on from my second husband. Paul and I were married for more than two years. It was a rocky on-and-off-again relationship, though we had an incredibly

CHAPTER SIX

strong connection that was extremely difficult to break. I knew early on that this relationship was not healthy for me, yet I just couldn't let go.

In my daily contemplations, I asked over and over for guidance to help me for my highest good and give me answers. Then I had two dreams. In the first one I had a huge book in my hands. Each page had about 20 pictures, front and back. The book was like a photo album, and was about 15 pages long. In the dream I "heard" that each picture represented one lifetime with Paul. Then the dream ended. From that dream I became aware that the strong connection we had for each other was because we had so many lives together. Even with that knowledge, I couldn't release the relationship. Until I had the second dream.

In this next dream I was shown that Paul rescued me from slave labor thousands of years ago. That act saved my life, and inwardly I made a pact to repay him for his help.

In that past life I distorted the idea of "help" to mean taking on inappropriate responsibility for him, which was not healthy for him or me. By having that dream, I got the courage and insight that the highest and best thing I could do for both of us was to end the relationship and stop taking on his responsibilities. I grew in wisdom and spiritual love from my marriage, even though it ended in divorce. My understanding of my past lives with Paul helped me navigate that relationship for my highest good.

In summary.

How do these different kinds of dreams help you? Well, for me they help guide my actions, help clear up worry, and show me a direction for my highest good in the most efficient way possible, thus helping create more positive karma. Bear in mind everything that happens in your life is to help you grow in more love, wisdom, and awareness. Nighttime dreams, waking dreams, recurring dreams, and Soul experiences such as lucid dreaming are guiding you to help elevate every part of your life.

CHAPTER SIX

Personal Notes

Personal Notes

7

Reincarnation

A few years ago I was giving a talk about the power of thought to a local church during their service. It was a small, tight-knit Christian congregation, but the members were open to non-traditional topics. To the best of my knowledge, this church did not teach reincarnation.

Right after my talk and the service ended, a little black girl about five years old came up to me and said, "You were my husband in my past life." After she said this to me, a middle-aged white woman, she ran off. I approached her later in the room where the congregation gathered for coffee and snacks. She acted shy around me and seemed not to know who I was.

What transpired between me and this little girl is quite common with little children. Many times when you ask small children, "what you were when you were big?", they will remember parts of their past lives, like this little girl did. I didn't ask her about reincarnation or past lives, nor did I say anything about it in my talk. Something inside of her prompted her to share this with me, before what I call the veil of awareness got shut down.

This chapter contains several examples related to

me by others about how they came to believe in reincarnation. Here some examples of how children can tap into themselves as Soul and realize and remember their past lives.

Jacqueline's story.

It was September 11, 2007, and I was driving my three year old son to pre-school. We were about to pass his favorite place – the fire house – and he asked, "Why does the fire truck have its ladder lowered over the street with the flag on it?" Wondering how to explain this to a three year old, I began to explain how six years ago, a terrible thing happened in New York City, where two planes flew into two very tall buildings full of people. As soon as I began to explain further, my son interrupted me, casually stating "Oh, I know, we saw everybody floating up to us all at the same time." After a brief moment of silence – during which I felt every hair on my body stand on end – my son quickly changed the subject, and left me utterly speechless and in shock! My son never mentioned it again!

As I mentioned before, when children are young they haven't yet fully disconnected from their spiritual roots. So you can often catch them remembering their past lives or lives between lives. They may blurt things out and quickly forget what they have said.

Dawn's memory of part of her past life, though, stayed with her for many years. Here is her story.

Dawn's reincarnation experience.

When I was about four years old, I did some things

CHAPTER SEVEN

my mother believed to be signs of reincarnation. On several occasions, I told my mother in great detail that she was doing things wrong in the kitchen and in performing house chores. This was because my "other mother" had taught me the correct way to prepare a meal and do chores. This happened quite frequently, to the point that my mother would ask me how my "other mother" would do something. This amused my mom and confused her at the same time. My mother knew what my experiences were in my first four years. Therefore, she concluded, I must have been reincarnated from a previous life.

As time went by these memories of my "other mother" seemed to fade. I no longer corrected my mother regarding cooking in the kitchen or house chores.

My mother will tell you that the only explanation for me knowing how to make meals and clean the house was that I was reincarnated. My mother does regret that she did not ask me questions, especially about who my "other mother" was and who I appeared to be in a prior life. In hindsight, I believe that my "other mother" was with me for longer than I realized.

I did not have a great childhood. Times were tough in so many ways for me and my sisters. To this day my mother will tell you I was the mother in the family. I think that was because of my "other mother'" who gave me the inner strength to be a survivor. I love her for that. These incidents are very clear to me. I still feel her presence from time to time. I know that my "other mother's" love lives on in me.

Why reincarnation? How does this knowledge affect your present life?

For Dawn, knowing and remembering her past life with her "other mother" helped Dawn get through a very hard childhood. But for many of us in the West, reincarnation is not part of our culture. Realizing that there is more than one lifetime to learn and grow as Soul should come as a comfort. If you don't get it right this time around you will be given more opportunities to develop. Also, like Dawn, we can bring awareness and knowledge into this lifetime from our past lives.

I have talked a lot about karma, but not much about reincarnation. The two go together like a hand and glove, and it is hard to talk about one without the other.

As I have previously written about karma, you have been exposed to the knowledge that all your thoughts, words and deeds create. You created your present life from your past lives' actions. The resulting effects include all the circumstances you were born into. This includes what kind of physical body you have, your gender, your family, your nationality, and your talents.

Reincarnation is exacting in what it provides you as Soul what you need to experience in this lifetime. There are no accidents, and there are no victims. This may be hard to absorb. There can be no victims if people create the backdrop for the situations that they find themselves in from past actions.

Reincarnation helps you understand why some people are born with deformities, or others are born geniuses, or others are born into certain cultures, nations, and monetary situations. It can explain why you have an instant affinity for some people and for others, not so much.

Some Souls have a choice in the manner and circumstances of their birth. These Souls have earned this right by their actions and consciousness from past lives.

For most Souls, their placement in the world was chosen for them by a Spiritual group called the Lords of Karma, who look for the best possible chance for an individual to develop a larger capacity to love. Think of the Lords of Karma as guides with complete authority to direct and pick your next incarnation based on your karma. They want the best possible spiritual opportunity for you. It is not necessarily the easiest. What you do with that lifetime opportunity is totally up to you.

Life between lives.

There is also life after your physical body dies. Life is continual. You as Soul are eternal. What you experience when your body dies is totally contingent on your state of consciousness at the death of your physical body.

There are many realms or levels of what people call heaven. Each realm has its own vibration, and you take on finer energy bodies in these higher heavens. Those bodies are what Soul needs to be able to handle the specific density of the place, just as our physical body here helps Soul endure the denseness of this physical reality.

At night while we sleep, many, (if not all) of us journey into these inner realms and interact and partake of life there. Many times we go to spiritual schools to learn the finer aspects of the complexities of life. Or we go to specific places on the inner worlds to help ourself with a problem here.

Two very interesting books talk at length about what happens after the death of your body though they provide only a partial picture. The two books are Life between Lives and Journey of Souls by Michael Newton.

Now that you have a little more understanding of reincarnation and what may happen after your body dies, let's focus on helping you use this lifetime to its best advantage. It is always best to live in this NOW because you can only create and change in this present moment, regardless of what your past lives had been.

Relationships: Why you are where you are.

Let's start with your family. The dynamics of your family show you so much of why you came into this particular group and what you may need to learn in this lifetime.

Take my situation. Youngest of eight, sick mother, very religious father. I was unceremoniously handed a lot of responsibility at a very young age. My brothers and sisters as a whole, were not a tightly-knit group so I couldn't expect a lot, if any, emotional support from them.

I was placed in this lifetime to for the opportunity to develop spiritually as much as I could. Everything that happened in my family relationships was my choice of

CHAPTER SEVEN

how to act and react. I could have chosen a thousand different directions that would have created a multitude of different outcomes.

Since I have the wisdom of hindsight, I realize the actions I did take helped me grow in a truer sense of responsibility. The circumstances, which were hard, help me grow in compassion and awareness. Even my mother being sick all the time taught me to be mindful of my health and my father's dogmatic religiosity helped spur my own spiritual searching.

I could have chosen to wallow in victimhood and never progress past the obviously dysfunctional family structure I found myself in. My inner knowingness about reincarnation helped me approach my life with different actions and thoughts than I would have if I didn't believe in it.

This is because I knew that my life was not just random. I intrinsically comprehended that living has a deeper purpose than only taking care of physical needs, and that all actions have consequences. Thinking back to the time as a teen, when I checked out the butcher knives and contemplated suicide, my inner realization about reincarnation and karma saved me. My inner spiritual voice told me if I took the route of suicide I would have to come back in my next life and face what I was unwilling to face in this life, and it would probably be harder.

How to recognize past life karmic relationships and lives.

Everything has a spiritual purpose, each and every encounter! You have probably shared different lifetimes with many people in your family, close friends, and romantic partners. Usually your closer relationships are ones where you have shared one or multiple lifetimes, like I did with my second husband Paul.

This is a memoir of a past life and how it helped Rose to confront what she needed.

Rose's story.

Sometimes you have to do what you have to do. For me, this was stepping out of an abusive marriage. I asked inwardly for help, and I received this inner experience.

I was a knight and leader in the First Crusades. Before heading out on our quest, I saw myself seated upon a horse in full armor. I was addressing a crowd of men before me. We were in a courtyard, and in the background was a large stone building a castle-like structure. The men were listening intently to me. I was giving a talk, preparing them for what they were about to experience.

I then saw myself on horseback. Riding on either side of me were two other knights. Armies of men followed behind us. Some were on horses, and many were marching by foot. We were on our way to Jerusalem to fight an important battle.

CHAPTER SEVEN

Soon I found myself amidst the battle Many men were killed. There was plunder and bloodshed everywhere.

The scene changed, and I was in the throne room of a castle. The room was large, and the walls were about 30 feet high, floor to ceiling. There were 10 or 12 individuals in this room. Honors were being bestowed upon me for completing my mission on the battlefield.

The scene changed again. The last moments of my life were revealed. I was on my deathbed. I felt resigned and ready to make the transition.

The lesson I learned in that lifetime was that I was brave!

Having this past life recall was very timely for me. It gave me the insight that I have had the direct experience of being truly brave and that I could draw upon it at any time in this life when I didn't feel so brave. It was the boost I needed to move forward in this life, as it resurrected a much-needed confidence I needed to finally step out of my abusive relationship.

Learning about your past lives can help you heal and give you the insight necessary to move forward when you find yourself stuck or at a loss about what to do. But just learning about the circumstance of a past life will not necessarily relieve the situation right away. You still may have to do the work, as I did with Paul and as Rose did. What we learned, helped us understand how to proceed in the best and highest way in this life.

Many times we are shown parts of past lives through our dreams or meditation, as was the case with Sandra.

Sandra's story.

When did I believe reincarnation was real? When did the fantasies of my day and night dreams stop being fantasy and become reality? It had something to do with trees.

There were still many untouched forests in our region when I was growing up. Shopping meant long car rides watching the trees flash by – creating a natural strobe effect against the light of the setting sun. It was then I would see, or rather perceive, the lives of native people who found their survival in these dense woods. These glimpses were so real to me that I felt I was there, living among them.

I saw similar images when I was at play by myself. I used to love to run, run, run and play hard, as much as I could push my little girl's body. There's a type of sight that our spiritual nature has, where you "see" yourself from within. There were times when I looked at myself with these "inner" eyes, and saw my legs as those of a male youth, longer, stronger and tanner than my legs were, physically. I wondered at this, although it never bothered me in any way. It seemed perfectly natural.

Many experiences later, I found myself learning a form of meditation with an older acquaintance. She had flute music playing on her record player. Very shortly after that, I found myself "melting" into a big arm chair. And then the music, the chair, and the room were all gone, and I was in another place and time.

I was sitting on a seat of logs, a bright and warm fire

crackling before me. My best friend in the world was sitting near me, playing a wooden flute. We talked and laughed. My thoughts were filled with the memories of our adventures together. We were both Native American youths who grew to be young men.

The experience only lasted what felt like a few minutes, but in it I knew his whole lifetime, right up to that moment. It was the happiest day of his life, knowing that the next day was his wedding day. Youthfulness giving way to the new adventure of adulthood.

Contemplating the experience, I realized all the connections I'd felt in the previous years. I'd experienced glimpses of a reality I had already known, and in fact still know and experience to this day. There were many lives, many different individuals I experienced, yet I am always the same "me" inside. It explained how I knew things at a young age that I couldn't possibly have learned in the few short years of childhood, that I gleaned from an accumulated learning over many lifetimes.

Recognizing a past life.

How do you recognize that this indeed, is a past life? For me there are two ways. One is a true knowing, like the dreams I had about Paul. You just know! I can't describe it in any other way. You just know, as Sandra did. Another way I recognize it is when I dream of a time period that is vastly different from the present day, which helps me notice the dream may be about a past life.

Take notice the next time you have a dream where

the setting is in the past, (like the middle ages) or from a time periods before you were born. These could be clues to your past lives. Write down the dreams. Find the message the dream is trying to impart. Trust your intuition. The more you trust it, the stronger it becomes.

A simple spiritual exercise you can do to remember your past lives through your dreams is by reciting the word mana (pronounced "mah-nah"). This mantra attunes you with the Causal Plane, the region of past-life memories. Remembering past lives takes practice. You will be shown past lives if you need to see something for your growth, but most of the time you have to ask. By putting your attention on past lives you are in effect asking for this awareness.

Besides relationship issues, continual health, financial, or consistent problems (like addictions) may be based in past lives. I had a client who is afraid of flying and is claustrophobic. Being in airplanes and elevators triggered feelings of being trapped. Through her own spiritual work she came to know she was a slave in ancient Egypt and was buried alive with her master. With this knowledge she is making progress on her fear. Knowing their origins helps her understand why she feels the way she does.

Working with the knowledge of your past lives is one way to help you understand and possibly heal issues you are facing. Knowing about a past life is just the beginning of healing, a starting point. You may still have to change your thinking and do emotional healing.

Also ask what spiritual lesson you need to learn

through your problem. All lifetimes are a spiritual school, packed with opportunities and lessons to help you to evolve in your capacity to love yourself and to give love to others. In essence every problem or circumstance is a chance to face what you need to face within yourself as Soul.

Deja vu.

When I was 18 I wanted to get away from my hometown of Rochester, New York and start fresh. I wanted a small to mid-size city where I knew no one. I was contemplating San Francisco, Denver, and Atlanta. There was no Google back then, so I relied totally on what others said about those cities and what climate they had. (Not a lot of research to be sure, but heck, I was 18.)

I picked Atlanta. Denver had winter, which I hate, and San Francisco, my brother told me, was always cold, too. So they were out. I worked at the time as a cocktail waitress and many of my customers had visited Atlanta and said they loved it. By default Atlanta won, though I had never been to either the city or the state of Georgia.

So off I went to Atlanta. I had no job lined up, I didn't know anyone, and I was driving there in a questionably safe car all by myself.

Though I had never been to Georgia, when I crossed the state line I began to sob almost uncontrollably, and I said to myself out loud, "I have come home!" There was only me in the car, and my outburst even surprised me. What I was experiencing, unbeknownst to myself at the time, was deja vu. In a past life I did live in Georgia, but when I was moving there I was not conscious of that possibility.

The feeling or sense of deja vu, like I experienced, can be an indication of a past life connection to a particular place. While I was writing this chapter I met a friend for coffee and got a very direct nudge from the Divine. During the conversation she asked what chapter I was working on now. I told her reincarnation. She looked right at me and very directly asked if I was going to write anything on deja vu. It just so happened that before I met her I had stopped writing at the heading of deja vu! I knew this was a message from Spirit.

I then asked her if she had any stories from her own life about this subject. Her eyes lit up and she said, "I have a very compelling one." Well, after all these "coincidences," I just had to put her story in this book.

Siobhan's story on deja vu.

I am an artist who from childhood had a passion for art and later Plein Air painting.

Sometime in the late 1980s, I went on a family vacation to Nantucket Island. I became fascinated by a small village at the very end of the island called Siaconset. In particular, I was drawn to a place called the Summer House. I convinced my family to take me there. I had no prior knowledge of this village. I did not read any of its history beforehand.

My family stayed in the car while I ventured into the main Summer House guest building. When I walked into

CHAPTER SEVEN

the lobby, I was overwhelmed with a feeling of having been there before. I knew this place. I knew Siaconset village. The manager asked as the feeling overwhelmed me, "You have been here before, haven't you?" I said, "Yes, I have."

Twenty-plus years later, I was visiting a French family in Nancy France. They lived across the park from the Ecole des Beaux-Arts, a famous art school there. After dinner, the family always took a grand walk in the early evening. As we walked out the front door, I glanced down the street. For the second time in my life I was overcome. The moment was stunning. I recognized this street. I had been on this street before. It was so strong a feeling that I had to stop. l was in tears.

One snowy winter night several years later, I decided to investigate why I had experienced deja vu twice. The internet made my research possible. Incredulously, there was a connection. Siaconset at the turn of the century was a haven for New York actors escaping the summer heat. It was also a haven for Plein Air painters as well. My research found a brief article written about a person's memory of her summers there. There were two sisters who visited the island and were artists. Their last name was Cowles.

That led me to investigate the name to find more. At that time, there was no ancestry.com, and my search for them ended. However, the name brought up an art school in Boston, the Cowles Art School, founded by a young artist in the late 1800s, named Frank Cowles. He had studied art abroad in France and had established *his school in the fashion of the Ecole des Beaux-Arts in Paris. I also read that the Cowles Art School had a sister school with which it exchanged art students. The Ecole des Beaux Arts in Nancy, France.*

There can only be one explanation. I am the person in that past life who travelled to both places. I am gratefully carrying on their passion for art and Plein Air painting in this life.

This experience of deja vu for Siobhan helped her realize why she was so compelled to study art and Plein Air style of painting. Through her research and her personal experience she has developed more clarity about reincarnation.

Animals are Soul, too.

How Andrew came to realize reincarnation and that animals are Soul.

I grew up in an African family where reincarnation was an accepted concept. For instance, the family elders would pay attention to the mannerisms of a new family member during their first three years to determine which "ancestor has returned." I didn't pay much attention to these concepts until my first personal experience.

In my teens, I was given a cat named Max who quickly grew attached to me. He had physical and behavioral traits that made him special for me. For instance, the following traits, easily missed by many, caught my attention: a crescent moon-like spot on his lower back, a preference for chicken instead of tuna, a fear of red

CHAPTER SEVEN

lights, and an attraction to blue lights.

Sadly, a year after getting him, he died due to my neglect. I felt much guilt and was so heartbroken that I cried for many days. One night, from the depths of my sadness, I asked God to please give me another chance at caring for a pet.

Less than a month later, while visiting a friend, I noticed his cat had just welcomed a litter of six beautiful kittens. As I got closer to the litter, one cat particularly caught my attention: the one with a crescent moon-like spot at the same location as Max had! Right at that moment, my friend said "I cannot handle this whole litter, I have to let a few go for adoption. Would you like one or two?" I could not believe my eyes and ears! "Yes", I said, "I'd like this one," pointing at my new Max. The cat was a female, so I named her Luna due to the crescent-shaped spot that reminded me of Max.

As Luna grew I kept my promise to do better with caring for a pet. I also noticed that she had the same mannerisms I saw in Max: an aversion to tuna and red lights, and an expressed preference for chicken and blue lights. For me, it was a sure sign that Max reincarnated to give me another chance to do right and enjoy our bond of love a bit longer than the first time.

Andrew learned so much through realizing his kitty reincarnated: How to love more, that all actions have consequences, and that life is eternal, even for animals who are going through their own journey as Soul.

In Summation.

You can acknowledge reincarnation as a simple fact or use this information for your development, as the people in these stories have shown. Daily life can be mundane or an exciting adventure based on your perspective and actions. Please take the realization of reincarnation and explore how it can benefit every aspect of your daily life.

CHAPTER SEVEN

Personal Notes

Personal Notes

8

Freedom and Awareness through Spiritual Exercises

Alone yet again! I left my first marriage with only my clothes, my car, and my job. Leaving my first husband in my early 30s was a hard pill to swallow even though I knew that our relationship was at an end and that I needed to move on for my growth and development.

Leaving my first marriage mirrored what I went through as a teen when I ran away from home. The similarity of being totally alone and losing so much was gut wrenching. Lucky for me, a friend had a home with a spare bedroom that she graciously allowed me to occupy, but living at my friend's house meant I couldn't take my cat. Much to my chagrin, I left my beloved kitty behind with my soon-to-be ex-husband.

With this sudden shift in my circumstances, I felt my whole world collapsing. I found myself one afternoon on the bathroom floor of my friend's house crying my eyes out, wondering why, yet again, I was going through such loss.

Understandably, I felt depressed and rudderless.

I did my best to navigate my divorce and my new

environment. Frankly, most of the time, I barely remembered going to work and trying to help clients. Though, truthfully, my clients were a saving grace for me, because by giving to others I was taking the focus off myself, even if only for a few hours.

My friend, Sara, who took me in, was a musician who played piano for a living at different venues, mostly at night. She was also working on creating her own music to sell and publish. Sara used a synthesizer keyboard to create a multitude of different musical sounds. It could recreate violins, horns, drums – almost any instrument you could name.

Her studio was directly across the hall from my bedroom. She was a night person, and I was up and perky at 5 am and sound asleep by 9:30 or 10. Like passing ships, we saw each other occasionally, mostly on weekends.

During this time, I was depressed and questioning myself constantly about the direction of my life. I was new to Eckankar and that was how I learned about singing HU to help me navigate life, the good and the not-so-good. So I learned, regardless of what I was going through, to chant or sing HU every day for nurturing, support, and strength.

After living at my friend's house for about a month, I went to bed at my normal time and was sound asleep by 10:30. Since Sara had gone to her job, I found myself alone in the house. Most of the time she rarely came home from her gigs before midnight or 1 am.

CHAPTER EIGHT

That night I was abruptly woken up by this incredibly loud and most gorgeous, breath-taking orchestral music I had ever heard. At first I thought it was Sara working on her musical arrangements. As much as I loved the music, I was also ticked off at Sara, to tell the truth, for being so disrespectful of my sleeping. I got up, ready to complain to her, but when I walked across the hall to her studio, I found it empty and dark. No Sara! No Sara anywhere in the house! Then the music abruptly stopped. I realized the angelic music I had just heard was indeed not from this Earth.

I was given a gift, a miracle, of Spiritual music to help me through my present trauma and upheaval. I felt internally grateful and amazed. I knew now I would come out of this hard phase of life ok. I was able to understand the meaning of this Divine message, which I felt was the direct result of the Spiritual work I had been doing consistently.

Being persistent in implementing Spiritual exercises helps you plug into help, wisdom, and nurturing, that can transcend mere physical needs. Spiritual exercises are food for you as Soul. This kind of help is there for all people of any belief system.

Using Sound as a Spiritual exercise.

Have you noticed how different songs or hymns can open your heart and inspire you? Working with Sound as a spiritual exercise helps you to inwardly attune your consciousness to a higher spiritual awareness. The process is very similar to how a musician uses a tuning device to find the right pitch for a musical instrument.

Certain Sounds bring you to different realms of consciousness and spiritual understanding.

Sound has been used throughout history for uplifting the individual. An example would be various people of different religions, such monks, chanting holy names or other mantras.

I have written about the HU in previous chapters. I will delve deeper now about using the Sound of HU as a Spiritual practice. HU is an ancient name for God and a pure carrier of Divine Love. When you sing it silently or out loud you create a connection to the Divine. By continuing to use the HU, you come into better harmony, unwind negative karma, and raise your awareness so you can be more in alignment with Spirit as you go about your daily life with more insight and balance (thus, hopefully, not so ready to create negative karma.)

The Sound of HU is the Sound of all Sounds. It has all the Sounds of Spirit contained in it. By singing it from your heart, either out loud or silently, you are in communion with the Divine of all life.

How to use the HU.

Find five, ten, or twenty minutes a day. Sit or lie quietly and softly sing HU. Don't direct it. Open your heart to it much like you would accept sunshine. You cannot direct the sun, but you can be open to receiving its light. After you have been doing this regularly, notice the subtle and sometimes not-so-subtle shifts in how you are thinking and acting and what is transpiring around you.

Another way to use the HU is to sing it silently be-

CHAPTER EIGHT

fore you go to sleep. You can ask inwardly for Spirit's help about a life situation before, during or even after you have sung the HU. Or you may want to be guided to the inner planes or heavens to garner greater clarity, perception, and understanding about a situation you are going through, or you may want to experience what lays beyond the physical.

Your dreams and your inner searching may be impacted by your singing the HU. Write down your dreams in the morning. They may give you clear windows into the answers or experiences that you seek. See how you feel, and notice any insights or how your dreams may be changing as you continue to do this at night.

Use the HU when you are around people that are "Debbie downers" if you really don't want to absorb their energies or get caught up in their conversations or situations. When you sing the HU for this reason, you are not trying to change anyone, you are working with the the HU to lift your own state of consciousness above any negativity.

When life is hard or you are going through a particularly rocky patch, find the time to be quiet and connect with this Divine energy. Know that by using the HU, you will begin to have a higher understanding of your problems and will help calm the emotional side of yourself. With this perspective you can make better actions and decisions. Keep in mind that every situation is in your life to teach you to develop more love, even the uncomfortable ones.

For example, a husband, a wife, or a close relative or

friend can trigger anger or frustration faster than strangers can, at least for me. So when I find myself getting impatient with my husband or when a friend does something that irritates me, I try to remember to sing HU silently to myself. I ask inwardly while I am singing HU to be guided to what I am (hopefully) to learn from this circumstance and to approach this situation with more of a loving heart. Over the years, by doing this, my patience has grown. I find that I gain a higher awareness of why something is happening even in the most difficult or uncomfortable of situations.

If you don't do anything as a spiritual exercise but sing the HU daily, you are using the most powerful, heart opening, and beautiful gift of love. It can help you create transcendence and miracles in your life.

There is a free HU app available in the App Store. On it, there is a recording of thousands of people singing HU for 20 minutes. I listen to it in my car while I am driving; it helps me to be calm and centered regarding the "different" ways people drive, I use it also to help me fill up with spiritual food. Another way to use it is to sing HU along with the recording.

I have had people who get the HU app tell me that when they play it, sometimes they also hear bagpipes or a single note of a flute or other Sounds. There are myriad Sounds you can hear. All the Sounds you become aware of are connected to a level of consciousness and Divine communication.

Usually when you hear Spiritual Sounds no one else can hear them, like when I heard the humming Sound

CHAPTER EIGHT

as a child or the celestial music I heard that night at my friend's house. Another Sound you can experience is the roar of the sea, which is connected to the Astral Plane. Hearing tinkling of bells is an indicator or the Causal Plane. Running water and buzzing of bees are Sounds from the Mental Plane and Etheric Plane. A single note of the flute is indicating the Soul Plane.

Whatever Sounds you may experience are indicators of Spirit communicating to you, to uplift you and give you Divine Love.

Using different specific mantras.

Using mantras and the HU are forms of spiritual exercises. Spiritual exercises change and uplift your consciousness in any given moment. Like physical exercise, the more you use them, the stronger and more aware you become.

Chanting or singing a mantra produces a series of spiritual effects, hopefully drawing you closer to Divine Love. When you repeat a mantra either out loud or silently, it focuses your mind to a sharper point that when consistently used, can penetrate through ordinary thoughts to deeper spiritual awareness.

Every mantra will align you to the specific vibration it is attuned to. Sometimes you may want a very particular understanding, or you may be curious about the different inner worlds and what they could teach you. You may wish to experiment with some of these and see what transpires.

Here is a list of mantras that I learned studying Eckankar. Let your inner guidance direct you to what you may need at any given time,

Alayi - Physical Plane

Kala - Astral Plane, seat of emotions

Mana - Causal Plane, past lives

Aum - Mental Plane, mental teachings

Baju - Etheric Plane, subconscious

Sugmad - Soul Plane, also name for God

ECK - The voice of God, or SOUND Current

WaH Z - A spiritual name for Sri Harold Klemp, the Mahanta, the Living ECK master

Z - same as above

Divine Love - Unconditional, merciful love with which God (Sugmad) looks upon all creation

Holy Spirit - another name for ECK

Joy - Soul experiences Joy

Mahanta - Inner Guide or Wayshower and Light Giver

Be cognizant that while you are chanting or singing mantras you may also inwardly hear different Sounds that I have mentioned, like a flute, the wind, violins, water, or the buzzing of bees. You may also see different colored lights in your spiritual eye, which is located between your eyebrows. You may also just feel more at peace and centered. All are good. Most of the time when I sing a mantra I feel more "filled up" with inner peace.

CHAPTER EIGHT

One woman's experience.

There were about eight people singing the HU at a recreation center where I was the facilitator. After the HU song ends, about 20 minutes or so, I always try to have a conversation with the participants to gauge their personal experiences. If no one wants to share, that is absolutely ok, too.

On this particular day I asked if anyone wanted to share how the HU affected them. One lady said she kept hearing the buzzing of bees throughout the process. I told her that was yet another Sound of God. The sound of buzzing bees correlates to the Etheric Plane or intuition. When I hear a different Sound I place my attention on it and open my heart to accept the gift. It happens in your life to help you in some way, though you may not always be cognizant of how it is uplifting your consciousness or helping you.

Another practice you can do with Sound is to sit quietly and focus on your heart area. Breathe slowly and deeply and concentrate on eliminating the sounds around you, like the fan of the furnace or air conditioner, or outside noises like dogs barking or trees being blown by the wind. After a few moments, listen for inner Sounds. They may be a high chirping sound like crickets or (what I experienced as a child) a high wire humming sound. What Sound you experience in your consciousness is there to uplift, nurture, and help you to become less entangled in the negative aspects of your environment.

Spiritual exercises using imagination and visualization.

The two aspects of the Holy Spirit are Light and Sound. Light and Sound are aspects of Divine Love. You may be drawn to the Sound or the Light. Your experience will be unique to you because you are unique. Experiment and see which method gets results for you. Results can be anything from feeling more light hearted to having an insight on a problem or a calming of your mind. Watch, listen and notice the subtle changes in your awareness and intuition.

There will probably be times when you will need to switch up the spiritual exercise you have been doing to keep developing. As with anything you try to learn, you become more proficient when you are consistent with these exercises and their wisdom and energy becomes more embedded in your consciousness.

Let's investigate some exercise with Light.

If you are like me, you may find it's hard to ignore the different news feeds and social media that are vying for your attention. As I have said before, most of media are not your friends. Even if their intention is to communicate world events or trends, the vibration, energy, and content is mostly negative. They will drag you down emotionally, mentally, and spiritually if you keep allowing their messages into your psyche.

Here is a spiritual visualization I created to clear that negative energy from your inner self and protect you from absorbing it in the future.

CHAPTER EIGHT

Exercise to guard from the negative world social consciousness.

Sit in a quiet place and take several deep, slow breaths. You might want to sing HU softly for a few minutes to elevate your awareness. Next, imagine a benevolent spiritual guide coming to help you, radiating with Divine Love and wisdom. You give the guide permission to assist you in removing the energies you have absorbed from anything negative you have watched or listened to that you knowingly or unknowingly allowed to enter your mind or emotions.

As the process begins, maybe the guide pulls out all the dark, negative energies. The loving being might ask you to drink from a cup filled with Divine Love because where there is Divine Love no lesser energy can co-exist. Or you might be brought to a golden waterfall and be directed to stand under the light-filled sparkling water. As the light-water flows over you, see all the darkness of the pessimistic media being washed away.

Pick a process that resonates with you. Visualize and imagine the worldly negativity leaving you, by whatever means you choose.

After a few minutes you may feel or see some kind of lightening in your body or thinking or perhaps a new sense of peace will have settled into your being.

Next, imagine a beautiful dome of sparkling white light surrounding you. This will protect you in the future if you engage in reading about or watching world events.

At this point fill your heart with gratitude and end the visualization, unless you are experiencing something more from Spirit, just for you. The more you do this, the less likely it is that you will allow yourself to watch or read anything that could drag you down.

Clearing your consciousness of old negative karma, habits, and energy.

We all come into this life with negative karma. Also, through daily living, we accumulate habits and thinking that can create more bad karma. This exercise came to me during one of my contemplations to help me clear my limiting karma and energies.

Try this visualization if you want to move forward in any way. Remember all growth and change starts from within. Your inner change then affects your outer life. Your life is the summation of the state of your consciousness. One of my symbols for consciousness is a house or a building.

Sit comfortably and sing HU for a few minutes, silently or out loud. Next, imagine a house or a building that needs repair, renovations or a deep cleaning. See yourself tackling the project. You can visualize spiritual guides helping you in your enterprise.

If you are hauling off old, dirty, or broken things, place them in a big dumpster labeled Spirit. See your helpers taking the refuse away. In essence you are letting go of old thinking, emotions, and karma and releasing them to Spirit.

Next, image yourself redecorating or rebuilding

your house or structure. Fill it with Light, Divine Love, and Joy. Make the picture very bright.

Do this exercise consistently, for a couple of days or weeks, until you feel or experience a shift in the issue that was bothering you or until you sense a lightness in your being or more peace and love in your daily life.

Another exercise with the Light.

Here is another exercise I created for myself. Sing HU or any of the other mantras I have mentioned. After a few minutes, imagine yourself walking into a building. It is brilliantly white, so white it almost sparkles. You enter the building with quiet excitement. There is a staircase, and you eagerly walk up several flights until you sense you are on the floor that you feel the most in tune with.

You look up and down the hallway and see several closed doors. Notice the one with light coming from under it. As you approach the door you can sense spiritual expansion is behind this door. You open the door and step through into a world of incredible light and transcendence. Breathe in and absorb the wonderful energy. Allow yourself to experience anything else that may transpire.

Problem solving from the Spiritual perspective.

Many times problems occur in your life because you don't realize you are being bandied about by subconscious beliefs that no longer serve your higher good or because you are working off past life karma. Problems also occur because you are not aware of stepping into other people's space and freedom. These are just a few reasons you may have difficulties.

But when you approach your worries and issues from a higher spiritual perspective, many times you get answers and direction on how to proceed with more discernment and insight.

For example, when my first husband and I split, I inwardly asked Spirit why this had happened. I sang HU daily and kept my heart open for answers. After a few weeks I had a dream. In the dream I saw my husband, happy and healthy, going off to a university, and I saw myself going to a totally different school of higher learning.

I realized the schools in the dream represented spiritual paths. We were needing different spiritual learning and had to separate to fulfill our best lives for this go-round. This realization, which I achieved through the dream state, helped me let go of any attachments and assisted me in processing my emotions about our breakup faster and in a healthier way.

Spiritual exercise for health issues.

As you grow spiritually you may need to eat different foods than you ate before. Or you may need to find a new approach to fitness and vitality, or you may need a new or different healthcare practitioner.

When I am going through health challenges, I ask for guidance through spiritual exercises. Invariably I am led to the right health care practitioner, or I learn what I should do nutritionally. Or through connecting

CHAPTER EIGHT

with Spirit I may realize I am holding on to emotions or thought patterns that are interfering with my overall health.

This first exercise is to help you raise your awareness above your problem to gain a perspective as Soul or from an elevated spiritual viewpoint. I have used this visualization with clients to help them gain a higher awareness of their issues.

Sing HU, Z, or Divine Love silently to yourself for a few minutes. Next, visualize yourself above the Earth, or just above your body. Look down, and from this elevated perspective ask for clarity and understanding of your problem from the wisdom of your true self, Soul. Become aware of the different parts of your issue. Maybe you are being led to look at emotions, or belief systems. Expect answers or information about a next step in the direction you need to go. End the exercise when you see or feel or know something that has clicked for you.

As you move through your daily life listen to your inner nudges and intuition. Write down your dreams, as they may be the messenger for your answers.

Visualizing different colors also can help heal your physical and emotional bodies. Colors are light, and each emits certain vibrations. For example, the color orange helps the physical body, while a clear blue is for your emotional self.

Let's say you have a stomach issue or a pain somewhere in your body. When you have finished singing

HU, imagine clear, beautiful orange light on the part of your body that you would like to be healthier. Ask for your highest good and understanding as to what you need to learn. Do this for several days; you may even need to do this longer.

A couple of things might happen as you continue to work with these colors. You may hear from someone about a healthcare provider that you never considered or had overlooked. Or the issue that was bothering you may dissipate or go away all together. Or you might become aware of emotions that need to be processed or notice a thinking pattern that is destructive.

I worked with the orange light for a gut issue I was having. Several times a week, for about six months, I was in agony and clueless as to why. Then one day, out of the blue, I had this notion to get tested for food sensitivities.

The test results revealed that I was off the charts sensitive to dairy. I was shocked. I was convinced that I was not eating much dairy, but when I took inventory of all the milk products I was consuming in a day, I was truly amazed.

I stopped eating all dairy products immediately, and the pain in my stomach went completely away!

If you are going through emotional issues try imagining a blue light entering your heart or head. Ask for awareness and the next steps to help you process those emotions that have been causing problems for you. Or just breathe in the blue light, and let it soothe your psyche.

CHAPTER EIGHT

Lessen your anxiety through Spiritual exercises.

Anxiety is a vibration of fear. You can have anxiety for myriad reasons, such as beliefs you absorbed as a child in this life, your diet, or past life issues that are unresolved in this life, to name a few. So how do you ferret out the source of your disquietude?

Try working with the exercises in this book about changing your beliefs and emotions regarding what is causing your fear or anxiety. Pay attention to your dreams because they may give you some answers. Or use the general written Spiritual exercise for fear if you are unaware of what is causing your fear. You can also ask Spirit to help you let go of your fear or anxiety in your dreams. Working on letting go of your fear and anxiety in these ways may create a whole new insight to help you live with more peace and love. Also know, where there is love, fear or anxiety cannot enter or exist, so you may want to work with some visualizations to fill yourself up with love and self-acceptance.

Spiritual exercise to create a Divine Love "fill up."

I created this exercise for myself when I need a Divine Love "fill up." Sit quietly and sing HU for a few moments. Imagine a golden heart radiating Divine Love in front of you. See the light gently enter your heart area. Imagine this energy center opening like a pupil in your eye, dilating to allow more light and love into your being and your heart area. Quietly accept as much as feels good. (You are in charge as to how much love you allow in. Ask your inner guide to help you to find the right balance for you.) Notice how your body feels and how your thoughts may be calmer.

End the exercise when you feel a shift. This could be a feeling of warmth, a lightness in your heart, or a gentle calmness settling in your thoughts.

Be aware that when you experience inner change, it will affect your outer actions and your life. Notice if you feel guided to let go of certain thoughts, actions, or habits. Ask for continued guidance in living with more tranquility. Try not to invalidate these subtle shifts, as this will impede your growth. I also tell my clients to validate every positive change, no matter how small. The process of recognizing change actually speeds up your growth and increases your intuition.

In Conclusion: How to use this handbook for your highest good.

Truth is simple. Living higher truth is the challenge. By doing so, transformation happens.

I have purposely made this handbook simple to help you easily integrate the tools found in these pages. I encourage you to use them daily. Explore your dream world, recognize your limiting beliefs, clear stuck emotional energy, delve into what your past lives might have been, and discover your daily spiritual practice to eliminate negative karma and help you recognize and realize you are Soul.

Your daily life is a golden opportunity to connect with more Divine Love. The worlds and heavens exist because of this Divine Love. It is here, there, and everywhere. It is up to you to become more aware of its existence.

Connect with the miracles that are waiting for you!

May the Blessings Be!

Resources.

Follow me on Instagram - marian_massie

I am creating a community for questions and answers and helpful tips. I would love to hear about the miracles and realizations that occur in your own life.

HU App - App Store (free)

eckankar.org

Learn more about yourself as Soul and the Divine nature or your life through the Eckankar website.

Books that can be helpful.

The Power of Your Subconscious Mind by Joseph Murphy.

The Spiritual Exercises of ECK by Harold Klemp.

Life between Lives and Journey of Souls by Michael Newton.

Homecoming by John Bradshaw.

You are Soul and *Dancing with God* by Marian Massie

The Hidden Messages in Water Masaru Emote

Personal Notes

Made in the USA
Columbia, SC
28 March 2024